Editor

Sara Connolly

Editor in Chief

Karen J. Goldfluss, M.S. Ed.

Illustrator

Mark Mason

Cover Artist

Tony Carrillo

Art Coordinator

Renée Mc Elwee

Imaging

James Edward Grace

Publisher

Mary D. Smith, M.S. Ed.

TCR 3976

MW00386936

DAILY W...

Nonfiction & Fiction

Writing

Includes:

➤ *150 writing activities that target six writing traits*

➤ *engaging nonfiction and fiction writing topics*

➤ *writing prompts for additional practice*

➤ *standards and benchmarks*

Ideas and Content
Word Choice
Fluency
Voice
Organization
Conventions

Focused, fun writing practice every day!

Teacher Created Resources

Author

Ruth Foster, M. Ed.

Teacher Created Resources

6421 Industry Way
Westminster, CA 92683
www.teachercreated.com

ISBN: 978-1-4206-3976-6

© 2012 Teacher Created Resources
Made in U.S.A.

Teacher Created Resources

Table of Contents

Seabirds—The Lazy Pelican—Penguin Color—Bird Discovery!—Bird Tears—On the Beach—Something Wrong —The Suspect at the Zoo—Flying Vomit—The Ten Eyes—The Most Daylight—Interview from the Future—Where I Live—Details for the Alien—Sightseeing—The Great Wall—Setting the Table—Alien in the Kitchen—Fire Alarm Diary—100 Years in the Future—What Stopped Planes—Bread Danger!—Not on This Train!—The Worst Meal—Tanka

Old or Ancient?—Fast and Swift—Selling Words—Action Packed—Sound Words—Lost!—Insect Lesson —Bad to Good—Snake in the River—Third Grader Discovers Amazing Treasure—HOMES—No More Pizzas!—Giraffe Heart—The Face in the Window—Like a Tortoise—Like a Cheetah—The Right Name— Boy or Girl?—Hippo Keeper's Log—Pet Journal—Action!—Plane Down!—Mystery Item —The Dove and the Ant—Metaphor Poem

The Dodo—Seeing a Dodo—Super Bats—Vampire Bats—The Garden—The Octopus—Mood Poems— Night for the Fox—The Gorilla—Gorilla News—Stop, Drop, and Hold On!—Earthquake!—Here I Sit!—Dinner Party at the Farm—Death Valley—Pecos Bill—Head to Toe—What Was I Petting?—On This Date—What's on Top?—Thank-You Letter—What a Gift!—Travel Writer—Ice Hotel—Tongue Twisters

Open and Close—The 50-Pound Box of Candy—The Best Boarding—Board Advice—Bears—The Opposite—The Dog and the Wolf—Inside the Dog or Wolf's Head—The Bridge Painter—What Color?—Letter to the President—Silly Riddles—The Date Line—Australia Diary—Safety Talk—The Right Way—Tears of Laughter—The Funny Dog—The Penny—Finding Treasure—Game Action!—Bat, Ball, or Rope—The Best Tree—When Trees Were Young—The Musician

The Fastest—The Race!—The Days of the Week—Potatoes All Week—Story Start—The Crow and the Water Pitcher—Phone Manners—No Such Thing!—School Day —Dogs that Sniff—Pet Problem—Zoo Escape!—What Calf?—The Calf in the Barn—Crossing South Georgia Island—Staying Awake—Journey on Ice —Journey to Mars—Rhyming Poems—The Cheebra—Captain Cook—Treasure Hunt—Raining Frogs—Raining Fish—Blast Off!

A Capital Idea—Song and Movie Names—Facts About Butterflies—A Big Surprise—What Hour Is Our Train?—Glass Panes—The Tallest Mountain—Under the Bed—It's or Its—The Note—Big, Bigger, Biggest—The Tallest Tale—The Bet—Talking About . . .—What the Rhino Knows—It's Gone!—What Island?—Travel Shock—The Longest Hiccups—Stop the Hiccups!—Goose, Gooses, or Geese—Buy It!—Proofreading Marks—Tied up in Kelp!—Picture Poetry

Introduction

The written word is a valuable and mighty tool. It allows us to communicate ideas, thoughts, feelings, and information. As with any tool, skill comes with practice. *Daily Warm-Ups: Nonfiction and Fiction Writing* uses high-interest and grade-level appropriate exercises to help develop confident, skillful writers.

This book is divided into seven sections. Each of the first six sections focus on one of the following key writing traits. These traits have been identified by teachers as effective tools for improving student writing. The last section in the book offers a set of writing prompts to encourage further writing opportunities throughout the year.

Nonfiction and Fiction—Writing Traits Focus

IDEAS and CONTENT   **VOICE**

WORD CHOICE   **ORGANIZATION**

FLUENCY   **CONVENTIONS**

Daily Warm-Ups: Nonfiction and Fiction Writing uses a format that allows for flexibility in both instruction and learning. You may wish to begin with Warm-Up 1 and progress sequentially through all or most of the writing practices provided in the book. As an alternative, begin by introducing and modeling a specific writing trait that needs to be addressed. Students can then use the warm-ups within that section to practice and apply the trait as they complete each of the writing activities. Once the section is completed, continue working through the remaining sections based on the needs of the class.

With 150 independent warm-ups, there are plenty of writing opportunities to last the entire school year. As with any subject to be learned and mastered, writing should be continually practiced. With an arsenal of good writing techniques and an understanding of the writing process at their disposal, students can achieve a comfort level regardless of the writing task. Daily writing and guided practice using essential writing traits can help students reach a measurable level of success.

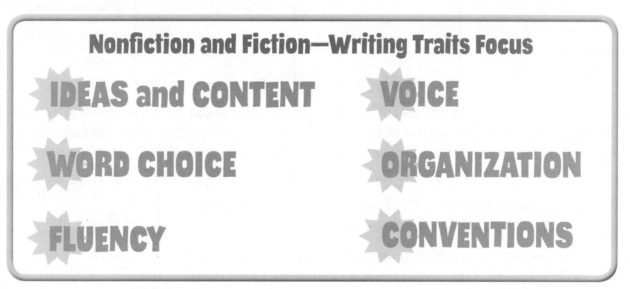

About This Book

The activities in this book were designed to help students gain experience writing in response to both nonfiction and fiction prompts. Each topic or theme includes pages that address both fiction and nonfiction writing.

Paired warm-up activities allow students to use both nonfiction and fiction writing on the same topic!

These paired warm-ups are about giraffes. The first warm-up presents nonfiction information and asks the writer to write a paragraph using the facts provided.

The second warm-up introduces the same topic in the form of a scenario and requires the student to write a story in the form of a fictional account.

The writing exercises in this book give students the opportunity to use a variety of writing formats. This allows a student to practice a specific writing skill while developing an understanding that good writing traits can be incorporated into a number of genres. The variation also keeps the daily writing activities exciting.

Each of the first six sections contains 25 warm-up writing pages that focus on the specific trait featured in the section.

The activities are written so that all students in a class can participate. While highly competent students may write more complex responses, all students will be able to practice writing at their respective levels of competence on a daily basis.

Each section ends with a page that incorporates both nonfiction and fiction writing activities. This page can be used as a culminating activity for the section, or as an informal assessment representative of the student's writing using the specific writing trait.

Space has been provided for students to write their responses on the activity pages. For instances in which students need additional space to complete an activity, use the back of the page, or continue on separate paper. Encourage students to use a notebook where they can extend their writing or create new writing pieces if they choose to do so.

The last section of the book includes a set of writing prompts that can be used throughout the year. These provide ideas, story starters, and a variety of scenarios for students to use as prompts. Students (or the teacher) can select one prompt a week to use as a topic for their writing. As an alternative, select a prompt and ask students to focus on one or two specific traits as they write. There are many ways to use these prompts. Choose a method that works best for you and your students.

Good Writing Traits

Ideas and Content . . . .

This trait lays the foundation for other aspects of effective student writing. Students need to learn to develop and organize their ideas and present them clearly. Students should gather their ideas, as well as research, seek new knowledge, and organize their information, before they begin to write. Successful writers write about what they know, the subjects in which they have expertise, or specific knowledge and experience.

In practicing the characteristics of this trait, students identify topics about which they have prior knowledge, investigate and explore topics further by conducting additional research if needed, and learn to connect their writing to their own experiences.

Writing that is strong in content includes interesting, relevant, specific details and a development of the piece as a whole. Students should have opportunities to practice organizing their ideas, writing about their own experiences, using examples and details, and writing complete pieces. This allows them to use insight and understanding to show readers what they know.

Word Choice . . . .

Paying attention to word choice enables students to write effectively so the reader will understand and want to read. Elements of the word-choice trait include using strong visual imagery and descriptive writing.

Writers learn to use accurate and precise words to say exactly what they want to communicate. Specific words convey distinct meanings. Students should use action words, as well as descriptive nouns and adjectives, to give their writing energy.

Using effective word choice implies a familiarity with the language as students learn to use parts of speech and subject-verb agreement properly. An effective writer listens to how words sound, using words that sound natural and add to the meaning of the writing.

As students become more adept at choosing the right words to express their intent, their written communication will be more easily understood and enjoyable to read.

Fluency . . . .

As students learn to incorporate the trait of fluency in their writing, they should continue to practice what they learned about the word choice trait. As writers develop fluency, they play with different word patterns and use words to match the mood of their writing. Fluent writing contains sentences varying in length and structure.

Students should learn to express themselves in clear sentences that make sense. This will happen as they incorporate natural rhythm and flow in their writing, making sure that ideas begin purposefully and connect to one another.

A writer may engage in a process of thinking that begins by asking the question, "What if?" One question leads to another, and the writer begins to develop smooth transitions and pacing. Mastery of each component of the fluency trait leads to a final outcome—the ability to pass a "read-aloud" test.

As students learn about the fluency trait, they should practice ways to express themselves by writing in a variety of formats. They will gather words to create word patterns and match specific moods.

Good Writing Traits (cont.)

Voice

As students gain confidence using the trait of fluency, they begin to learn about writing style. The voice trait focuses specifically on a writer's individual style. An effective piece of writing that exhibits aspects of the voice trait will sound like a particular person wrote it. Therefore, writing that has characteristics of voice will also be fluent; it will have natural rhythm. Authors develop their own unique style by writing from their thoughts and feelings. An author's personality comes through in his or her writing. Effective writers focus on their audience: They write to the reader. They want to call attention to the writing and draw the reader in. To do this, authors will write honestly, sincerely, and with confidence. As they write based on their own experiences and knowledge of themselves, writers will have the ability to bring a topic to life.

Students should continue to practice expanding their perspectives, as well as read sample pieces written from another person's point of view. By doing so, they will learn to identify elements of the voice trait in written samples and begin to develop their own style by writing reflections and personal correspondence.

Organization

Once students learn to incorporate the organization trait in their writing, they begin to view the whole picture. Effective writing has a logical order and sequence with clear direction and purpose; it does not confuse the reader. Rather, writing that displays qualities of organization guides the reader through the writing, leading to the main point. Writers who incorporate the characteristics of the organization trait include an introduction that captures the reader's attention and conclude the piece by making the reader think. Organized writing flows smoothly, with transitions that tie together.

Students can practice the characteristics of this trait by learning about beginnings and endings of stories and paragraph structure. They should practice writing their own paragraphs. The teacher can assist by introducing story elements to the students and giving them opportunities to outline a story, identify story elements, and write a complete story. As students learn to organize their written work, they begin to focus on appropriate pacing and transitions in their writing, leading to a more cohesive and readable final product.

Conventions

Students put the pieces together as they worked through the organization trait and began to consider the whole picture. They also had opportunities to consider self-evaluation, based on established criteria. The next major step in the writing process is editing. The conventions trait breaks the huge task of editing into smaller parts—allowing students to practice editing their own and others' work, focusing on one factor at a time.

Students learn about and practice correct forms of conventions, such as correctly spelling plural and singular forms of nouns, capitalization of place names, punctuation, possessives, and subject-verb agreement. While students often practice characteristics of the conventions trait by reading and editing samples written by others, it is important that they continually edit their own work.

Presentation

The trait of presentation refers to the publication part of the writing process. After students have completed a written piece, they present it to their audience: visually, orally, or using both formats. The presentation trait consists of two components: visual and auditory.

Students consider appropriate visual formats for their writing, as well as the use of color. Visual aids include charts, diagrams, and graphs. The visuals may include text. Specifically, students learn how to create a graph for a presentation.

The auditory component of presentation includes presenting work in an oral format; students learn public-speaking skills through drama and critique. Practicing this trait also gives students the opportunity to speak about a personal experience, ask and respond to questions, and clearly state their main point when presenting their writing to others.

 **A NOTE ABOUT PRESENTATION**

While presentation is not included among the sections of this book, its importance should not be discounted. The goal of the activities in this book is to provide relatively short, daily warm-up practice. The presentation process involves additional time and preparation. However, you can periodically allow students to display and present some of their writing to an audience with a focus on good visual and auditory techniques.

EVALUATING THE EFFECTIVE USE OF TRAITS IN THE WRITING WARM-UPS

As students work toward mastery of the writing traits and practice using them in their daily writing, it is important to assess their progress along the way. This can be done throughout the year. To determine whether a student is applying a trait to a particular writing piece, you may choose to evaluate the writing sample using a scoring rubric. Select those writing samples you wish to assess, and use one or more of the applicable writing traits to determine how well the student met the criteria.

A sample scoring rubric is provided on page 8. Each trait can be presented individually so that it can be used to help students as they first learn about the Good Writing Traits, or page 8 can be passed out in its entirety to serve as a reference.

Use each trait rubric by itself to score writing from that section or combine traits to match special assignments. You can also teach the traits in a cumulative manner, adding one trait to your rubric as you begin each section. Another option is to create your own descriptions using page 8 as an example. Yet another alternative is to include students in the process by creating a rubric with them based on their growing understanding of each trait.

Before using any rubric, make sure students are aware of the criteria for which they will be assessed. Model sample writing pieces using the trait and criteria prior to using the rubric as a tool for evaluation. Keep in mind that a rubric is flexible and can be adapted for specific writing practice or group warm-ups. It is an effective and relatively quick way to assess student progress.

Sample Scoring Rubric

	4	3	2	1
Ideas and Content	The writing has a clear central idea, and it is supported by vivid details.	The writing has a clear central idea but it doesn't have many details supporting it.	The writing has a developing central idea; details may be focused on another idea.	The writing does not have a clear central idea; there are not enough details, or the details are not related.
Word Choice	The writer chose the most clear and engaging words for the meaning and purpose.	The meaning is clear, and some of the writer's word choices are engaging and match the purpose.	While the meaning is clear, the vocabulary is very basic or is not a good choice for the purpose.	Words are used incorrectly, or the vocabulary is too limited to show the meaning.
Fluency	Sentence length is varied and the writing flows well.	The writing is readable, and in some parts, the writing flows well.	The writing is readable but does not flow.	The writing can be read aloud only with practice.
Voice	The tone is engaging and the writing was thoughtfully created for a specific audience.	The writing was obviously intended for a specific audience.	The writing is generic; it is not engaging and it may not be clear who the intended audience is.	The writing is not appropriate for the audience.
Organization	The writing is organized clearly, and it logically moves the reader through the text.	The writing is organized; the structure makes sense, though there are better alternatives.	There was an attempt at organization, but the writing would make more sense in another structure.	There is no clear structure. Events and information seem random.
Conventions	Even, appropriate conventions make the writing clear and readable. Errors are few.	The writer has control of the basic conventions. There are some errors, but they are not distracting.	The writer has made some mistakes consistently throughout. Errors are distracting.	Errors make the writing difficult to read. The writer incorrectly uses basic conventions.
Presentation	The writing is neat, and the visual elements add appeal. If read aloud, it is read in a practiced, engaging manner.	The writing is neat and readable. The visual elements are not distracting.	The writing is readable. It can be read aloud clearly.	Presentation is distracting or messy, making the meaning unclear.

Meeting Standards

Each activity in *Daily Warm-Ups: Nonfiction & Fiction Writing* meets at least one of the following standards and benchmarks, which are used with permission from McREL. Copyright 2012 McREL. Mid-continent Research for Education and Learning, 4601 DTC Boulevard, Suite 500, Denver, Colorado 80237. Telephone: 303-337-0990. Website: www.mcrel.org/standards-benchmarks. To align McREL Standards to the Common Core Standards, go to www.mcrel.org.

Uses the general skills and strategies of the writing process

1. Prewriting: Uses prewriting strategies to plan written work (e.g., uses graphic organizers, story maps, and webs; groups related ideas; takes notes; brainstorms ideas; organizes information according to type and purpose of writing)

3. Editing and Publishing: Uses strategies to edit and publish written work (e.g., edits for grammar, punctuation, capitalization, and spelling at a developmentally appropriate level; uses reference materials; excludes extraneous details and inconsistencies; selects presentation format according to purpose; uses available technology to publish work)

5. Uses strategies (e.g., adapts focus, organization, point of view; determines knowledge and interests of audience) to write for different audiences (e.g., self, peers, teachers, adults)

6. Uses strategies (e.g., adapts focus, point of view, organization, form) to write for a variety of purposes (e.g., to inform, entertain, explain, describe, record ideas) .

7. Writes expository compositions (e.g., identifies and stays on the topic; develops the topic with simple facts, concrete details, examples, definitions, quotations, and explanations; uses domain-specific or content area vocabulary; excludes extraneous and inappropriate information; uses logical organizing structures such as cause-and-effect, chronology, similarities and differences; uses several sources of information; provides a concluding statement)

8. Writes narrative accounts, such as poems and stories (e.g., establishes a context that enables the reader to imagine the event or experience; develops characters, setting, and plot; creates an organizing structure; uses transitions to sequence events; uses concrete sensory details; uses strategies such as dialogue, tension, and suspense; uses an identifiable voice)

9. Writes autobiographical compositions (e.g., provides a context within which the incident occurs, uses simple narrative strategies, and provides some insight into why this incident is memorable)

10. Writes expressive compositions (e.g., expresses ideas, reflections, and observations; uses an individual, authentic voice; uses narrative strategies, relevant details, and ideas that enable the reader to imagine the world of the event or experience)

12. Writes personal letters (e.g., includes the date, address, greeting, body and closing)

Uses the stylistic and rhetorical aspects of writing

1. Uses descriptive and precise language that clarifies and enhances ideas (e.g., concrete words and phrases, common figures of speech, sensory details)

2. Uses paragraph form in writing (e.g., indents the first word of a paragraph, uses topic sentences, recognizes a paragraph as a group of sentences about one main idea, uses an introductory and concluding paragraph, writes several related paragraphs)

3. Uses a variety of sentence structures in writing (e.g., expands basic sentence patterns, uses exclamatory and imperative sentences)

Uses grammatical and mechanical conventions in written compositions

1. Writes in cursive

2. Uses pronouns in written compositions (e.g., substitutes pronouns for nouns, uses pronoun agreement)

3. Uses nouns in written compositions (e.g., uses plural and singular naming words, forms regular and irregular plurals of nouns, uses common and proper nouns, uses nouns as subjects, uses abstract nouns)

4. Uses verbs in written compositions (e.g., uses a wide variety of action verbs, past and present verb tenses, simple tenses, forms of regular verbs, verbs that agree with the subject)

5. Uses adjectives in written compositions (e.g., indefinite, numerical and predicate adjectives; uses conventional patterns to order adjectives)

6. Uses adverbs in written compositions (e.g., to make comparisons)

7. Links ideas using connecting words (e.g., uses coordinating conjunctions in written compositions)

9. Uses conventions of spelling in written compositions (e.g., spells high frequency, commonly misspelled words from appropriate grade-level list; uses a dictionary and other resources to spell words; uses initial consonant substitution to spell related words; uses vowel combinations for correct spelling; uses contractions, compounds, roots, suffixes, prefixes, and syllable constructions to spell words)

10. Uses conventions of capitalization in written compositions (e.g., titles of people; proper nouns [names of towns, cities, counties, and states; days of the week; months of the year; names of streets; names of countries; holidays]; first word of direct quotations; heading, salutation, and closing of a letter)

11. Uses conventions of punctuation in written compositions (e.g., uses periods after imperative sentences and in initials, abbreviations, and titles before names; uses commas in dates and addresses and after greetings and closings in a letter; uses apostrophes in contractions and possessive nouns; uses quotation marks around titles and with a comma for direct quotations; uses a colon between hour and minutes; use commas for tag questions, direct address, and to set off words)

The Lazy Pelican

2

DID YOU KNOW?

A pelican is a seabird. It scoops up fish and water when it dives into the sea. How does the pelican get rid of all the water when it comes up? It tilts its head and dumps it out. That's when the pelican has to watch out. A frigate bird may swoop down, land on its head or beak, and steal the fish!

Activity: Write a story about a pelican. You can name the pelican any name you want. Tell how the pelican is lazy and never wants to move fast. Tell how a frigate bird teaches the pelican a lesson!

_____

_____

_____

_____

_____

_____

_____

_____

_____

_____

_____

Penguin Color

DID YOU KNOW?

Penguins are dark on the back and light on the belly. This helps protect them from orcas and sharks. Look down at a penguin swimming, and you will have a hard time seeing it. This is because the dark color blends in with the deeper and darker water. Look up at a penguin swimming, and it is hard to see. This is because the light color blends in with the lighter sky above.

Activity: Now it is your turn to describe an animal. When you write, first tell what animal you are describing. Then talk about its color and what it looks like. Why do you think it is colored the way it is?

_____

_____

_____

_____

_____

_____

_____

_____

_____

_____

_____

_____

_____

Bird Discovery!

DID YOU KNOW?

New bird species are still being found today. One new bird was recently found in Madagascar. The funny thing about this bird is that people knew about the bird for decades! They could tell it was a new bird because of its call. The bird stays hidden during the day. It only comes out at night. It is a type of rail that lives in dry forests. It is well camouflaged. Rails have long toes and strong legs for walking and running.

Activity: Imagine that you find a new bird species. Give your bird a name, then describe where the bird lives and what its habits are. What does it look like? What does it eat? How was it found?

This is your writing, so you can make your bird any way you like. It can be like a real bird, or it can be very odd and strange. Have fun with your imagination!

Bird Tears

THINK ABOUT IT!

Newspapers are full of stories called articles. People read articles for facts.

The title of an article is called a headline. Headlines should make someone want to read the story. A big and important article has a byline, which is the author's name.

Activity: Use the notes to write an article. Include a headline and your byline.

- Rio Del Mar Beach, Texas
- January 5
- visitor reported flock of crying birds
- park rangers said birds were Herring gulls
- said birds shedding tears but not crying
- all seabirds have special glands above their eyes
- gland helps remove extra salt from food and water
- salt comes out in tears
- tears run down beak, drip off end of bill

On the Beach

IMAGINE THAT!

Imagine something washing up on a beach. You are the writer, so it can be anything. It could be a boat, bird, shark, or whale. It could be a bottle with a message or a make-believe creature.

Activity: Write a newspaper article about it. Think of a headline that makes people want to read your story. Include your byline. Tell where, when, what happened, and why.

Something Wrong

What is wrong with this story?

> Frank was a great explorer. He went to the North Pole and saw lots of penguins. Frank saw an amazing thing at the North Pole. He saw penguins with eggs on their feet! If the eggs were on the snowy ground, they would freeze.

Hint: Almost all penguins live south of the Equator, and there are no penguins in the North Pole.

When writers write, they use what they know. If they don't know something, they ask questions. They look in books or use a search engine on a computer.

Activity: Write a paragraph like the one in the box above. Have all the facts right except for one thing. You can put an animal where it should not be, or you can have an animal doing something it cannot do. On the back of this page, write down what was wrong with the story. Have other people read your paragraph. Could they spot what was wrong with the story?

_____

_____

_____

_____

_____

_____

_____

_____

_____

_____

The Suspect at the Zoo

IMAGINE THAT! You are a detective. You are talking to a suspect. The suspect says, "I did not do it. I could not have done it. I was at the zoo. At the zoo I saw..."

Activity: Finish the suspect's paragraph. In your paragraph, use what you know about animals and zoos. Describe all the things you might see at a zoo. Describe what the animals are doing or look like. Have one or two animal facts wrong. Then have the detective say, "Your story cannot be true because . . ."

_____

_____

_____

_____

_____

_____

_____

_____

_____

_____

_____

_____

Flying Vomit

DID YOU KNOW?

An albatross is a seabird. Albatrosses sit on their eggs in nests. What if an albatross on the nest feels scared? What if it is afraid of what might be coming? Albatrosses have a special way of defending themselves. What will the albatross do? It will vomit up a jet of fishy oil! The oil flies several feet through the air. The oil really stinks!

Activity: Write about a time when you were really scared. Where were you? Who was with you? What were you doing? How did you feel? What did you do? Did you act the same as an albatross?

The Ten Eyes

Activity: Write a story about someone who is really scared. The person is scared of ten unblinking eyes. Describe the person and his or her surroundings. Is there someone else in the room? Use what you know about being scared to describe what the person is feeling and thinking. Then at the end of the story, tell what the ten eyes are—the moon shining on his, her, or someone else's toenails!

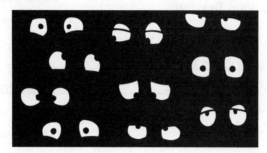

_____

_____

_____

_____

_____

_____

_____

_____

_____

_____

_____

The Most Daylight

DID YOU KNOW? You can ask people questions to find out things. This is called an interview. It is good to think up some questions before you start. This helps you find out what you want to know.

Activity: Write a dialogue between yourself and a scientist. The scientist studies the Arctic tern, a seabird. The Arctic tern sees more daylight than any other creature on Earth. Use the information in the box to think up some questions and answers.

Remember to put a colon (:) after the name of the person who is talking. (You can make up any name you want for the scientist.)

Arctic terns:

- migrate from Arctic to Antarctic and back every year
- can live up to 34 years
- may go 1,500,000 miles in a lifetime (this is more than three times to the moon and back)
- see more daylight because spend summer in each place
- may have tracking rings on them so that scientists can measure how far they have traveled

_____ :

(Your name):

_____ :

_____

_____

_____

_____

_____

_____

_____

_____

Interview from the Future

IMAGINE THAT! Imagine that you are grown up. You are being interviewed about your job or something you did. You are the writer, so you can do or be anything you want. You could have saved someone. You could have discovered something. You could have built or climbed something. You could be an astronaut or a firefighter. You could be a driver, an actor, a cook, or a dancer. You could be an artist, a scientist, or an athlete. You choose!

Activity: Write what was said in your interview. Remember to separate the name of the person speaking from what he or she says with a colon (:).

_____

_____

_____

_____

_____

_____

_____

_____

_____

_____

_____

_____

Where I Live

DID YOU KNOW?

Hundreds of thousands of seabirds can nest in one place. They nest on islands out in the ocean. This means there are few land predators. It also means there is plenty of wind for easy takeoffs and landings.

Where do you live? With whom do you live? Why do you live there?

Activity: When you write down answers to these questions, include lots of details. Details are bits of information. Your details may be about the city in which you live, the size and color of your house, or about the people who live around you.

Example sentences with details:

I live in a big city that is close to the ocean.

My house has seven floors, and it is red with black trim.

I live with my father who drives a truck to work.

_____

_____

_____

_____

_____

_____

_____

_____

_____

Details for the Alien

Activity: Imagine you are meeting an alien. The alien has never been to Earth and asks you where you live. Write a paragraph describing where you live. Include the name and one detail or more about your:

- planet
- continent
- country
- state
- city
- house
- room

_____

_____

_____

_____

_____

_____

_____

_____

_____

_____

_____

Sightseeing

IMAGINE THAT!

People visit new places and sightsee. They look at things that are new or different. They may look at bridges, buildings, trees, or mountains. They may visit museums or parks. They may go swimming or skiing. You know more about what one can do where you live than a visitor does.

Activity: Write a letter to someone who may visit you. In your letter, describe at least three things one can do or see where you live. Tell why these things are special. Tell why the person might enjoy visiting or doing these things.

Remember: Greetings and endings have their own lines in letters.

Dear _____ ,

Your friend,

_____

_____

_____

_____

_____

_____

_____

_____

_____

_____

The Great Wall

THINK ABOUT IT!

The Great Wall is in China. It was built long ago to help protect China's northern border. It stretches for thousands of miles. Today many people visit the Great Wall. There is a rumor about the Great Wall. The rumor started because the Great Wall is so big. The rumor is that the Great Wall is so big that it can be seen from the moon.

This rumor is not true. Imagine a human hair, then imagine standing two miles away. Could you see the hair? No, you could not! Looking at the Great Wall from the moon is like looking at a single human hair from two miles away.

Activity: Imagine you are going to China with a friend. Your friend wants to see the Great Wall because it can be seen from the moon. Write a letter to your friend. Tell your friend what is true about the Great Wall and why he or she still might want to see it.

_____

_____

_____

_____

_____

_____

_____

_____

_____

_____

_____

17

Setting the Table

Ideas and Content

THINK ABOUT IT! How do you set the table? What side of the plate does the napkin go on? Where does the knife go? It can be hard to remember the rules.

Activity: Write down how to set the table. Break it into steps. Start by writing a title that says what your how-to is for. Use the diagram to help. Remember to use words like *left*, *right*, *top*, *bottom*, *facing*, *in*, and *out*.

_____

1. _____

_____

2. _____

_____

3. _____

_____

4. _____

_____

5. _____

_____

6. _____

Alien in the Kitchen

IMAGINE THAT!

You know how to do many things. Imagine that an alien from Mercury has come to visit you. The alien wants to learn how to cook some Earth food. You tell the alien that together you will make tacos, pizza, hot dogs, or some other type of food.

The alien goes into a closet and takes out clothes. Then it goes to another closet and takes out a broom. The alien puts the clothes on the broom! Then it puts the broom under the bed. "It will be ready to eat in five days," the alien says.

Activity: Write a how-to for the alien. Plan ahead! In your head, think of what you will cook. Think of the things you will need. Then tell the alien what room to go to and where the things are that it should take out. Step by step, tell the alien what to do. Write a title for your how-to.

_____

_____

_____

_____

_____

_____

_____

_____

_____

_____

_____

Fire Alarm Diary

DID YOU KNOW?

People keep diaries to tell what happened to them. They say how they feel and what they saw. We can learn about the past from reading people's diaries.

One woman wrote a diary in 1836 when she was on the Oregon Trail. When she reached the prairie, she wrote about "leaving the timber." She wrote about using buffalo dung for cooking fuel. When she reached the mountains, she wrote about steep trails. She had to leave her trunk and walk single file.

Activity: Write a diary entry for a fire drill day. Start your entry with the date and location. Then tell all about the fire drill. Tell why you have them. Tell what they sound like. Tell what you do. Just imagine—someone reading your diary entry in 100 years might learn how things were different!

100 Years in the Future

IMAGINE THAT!

Imagine it is the future. You are the same age, but it is 100 years later than today!

Activity: Write one or two diary entries. Tell what you do, eat, and feel. Will you have a backpack that helps you fly? Will you be able to travel to Mars? Will you go to school? Use your imagination. It is your diary entry, so you get to write about a world you think up.

What Stopped Planes

DID YOU KNOW?

In April 2010, something happened that caused airlines to stop flying planes over western and northern Europe. What stopped the planes? A volcano had erupted in tiny Iceland. The eruption sent a huge ash cloud into the air. The ash was blown about and spread all over. It was not safe for planes to fly through the ash. Tiny bits of ash could harm the plane engines.

Planes were stopped on April 15th. Many people were angry that they could not travel. People got stuck in airports and trains got overcrowded. It was a mess! Planes were not allowed to fly for five days. People checked the news all the time to find out when they could fly again.

Activity: Write a newscast for this time. Tell people what happened. Tell them where, why, and what they should do. Tell people you will give up-to-date information. Start your newscast, "Hello, this is _____ with breaking news."

_____

_____

_____

_____

_____

_____

_____

_____

_____

_____

Bread Danger!

IMAGINE THAT!

Imagine that a baker makes too much bread dough. It won't stop rising! The dough begins to take over. It goes out the door and into the streets!

Yeast is what makes bread rise. What kills yeast?

- water that is too cold
- water that is too hot
- too much contact with salt

Activity: You are the newscaster describing the breaking news. Write your newscast. Tell what the problem is. Tell where it started. Describe how fast the dough is moving. Describe what is happening in the streets and city. Then, use the information in the box to tell people what to do or how the yeast is stopped.

_____

_____

_____

_____

_____

_____

_____

_____

_____

_____

Not on This Train!

DID YOU KNOW?

The durian is a fruit from Southeast Asia. Many people call the durian the "king of fruits." Other people think it is bad. This is because of its smell. Its smell is very strong. It makes some people sick.

What is the smell like? Some say it is rotten onions, turpentine, and gym socks. The smell lingers, too. (When a smell lingers, you can still smell it after it is gone.) The durian has been banned in many places. It cannot be taken on trains or into hotel rooms. It cannot be taken into hospitals.

Activity: What is your opinion about the durian? Is it okay to ban it? An opinion is how you feel about something. When you write your opinion, make sure you:

- tell what you feel
- describe the durian
- give reasons and examples that support your feelings

_____

_____

_____

_____

_____

_____

_____

_____

_____

The Worst Meal

Activity: Use your imagination to come up with the worst meal in the world. Use lots of details when you describe your meal. The only rule is that it has to be made from things that people eat. Remember, you cannot be wrong when it comes to the worst meal because it is your opinion.

When you write, be sure to mention:

- how it looks
- how it feels
- what it smells like
- what it tastes like

In some places people eat:

- bats
- scorpions
- spiders
- poisonous fish
- grasshoppers

_____

_____

_____

_____

_____

_____

_____

_____

_____

_____

Tanka

DID YOU KNOW?

Tanka is a kind of poetry. A tanka is an unrhymed Japanese poem that has five lines. Each line has a certain number of syllables. The lines have *5, 7, 5, 7,* and *7* syllables.

What is a syllable? Put your hand under your chin and say a word. Your hand will hit your chin every syllable. A syllable is the number of times you hear a vowel (a,e,i,o,u) in a sentence.

Activity: Write a tanka poem. Your poem can be about something real or made up. It can be about what a place is like, an animal, a feeling, or an imaginary thing. You choose! Be sure to count the syllables in each line.

Warning: this is harder than you think!

Tanka Poem Examples

The Joey	The Mermaids
The joey sticks its (5 syllables)	Deep underwater (5 syllables)
Head out and says I am a (7 syllables)	The mermaids play, sing, and dance. (7 syllables)
Baby kangaroo (5 syllables)	They have to watch for (5 syllables)
Safe inside my mother's pouch (7 syllables)	Nets and hooks, but they do not (7 syllables)
Hopping fast across the land. (7 syllables)	Ever have to wash their hair. (7 syllables)

_____

_____

_____

_____

_____

_____

Word Choice

Old or Ancient?

THINK ABOUT IT!

If one is old or ancient, one is not young. What word should a writer use: old or ancient? Does it matter? Yes, it does matter. This is because the writer can set a mood. The writer can help the reader feel a certain way. The writer can help the reader form a better picture in his or her head. "Ancient" makes one think of not just being old. It makes one think of things long, long ago. It makes one think of times long past.

Look at the word pairs. Pick the word in each pair that is old or ancient compared to the other word. Write it in the correct column.

a. grandfather   caveman   **b.** pyramid   log cabin

	old	**ancient**
a.	_____	_____
b.	_____	_____

The Mayan people live in Central America. Thousands of years ago, they created a written language. They made numbers.

Activity: Look at the Mayan numbers. On another piece of paper, write your age using the Mayan number system. Then write about what you did. Tell what numbers you used—were they old or ancient? Tell what each dot and line stands for. Then explain why it is easier to use modern numbers. Use an example of writing out a higher number in Mayan and modern numbers to prove your point.

0	1	2	3	4	5	6	7	8	9
10	11	12	13	14	15	16	17	18	19

fast and Swift

Think of all the words you can use for *fast*. Write some of them here:

_____

_____

_____

Activity: Now, write a story in which you use those words. In your story, have someone hear a noise. Have the person be scared. Have the person run away without seeing what is behind him. Make it sound as if it is a bad thing chasing the person. Then, at the end, have a surprise. Have the thing catch up only to help the person, tell him something nice, or give him something he dropped.

_____

_____

_____

_____

_____

_____

_____

_____

_____

Selling Words

THINK ABOUT IT!

Think of an advertisement. Words in ads are chosen carefully. Ads are written so that you'll want to buy what is being sold. They are written to make you want something and so you think something is the best, and so that you'll think what is being sold is worth the money.

Activity: Choose something to sell. It can be a game, toy, car, trip, or anything else you want. Write an ad for it. In your ad, describe what is for sale. Use words that will make it sound the best and make people want or think they need it.

_____

_____

_____

_____

_____

_____

_____

_____

_____

_____

_____

_____

Action Packed

Word Choice

THINK ABOUT IT! What if you want people to see a movie? You do not say the movie is good. You say it is fantastic, action-packed, or a heart-stopper. You say it will make you cry and keep you on the edge of your seat.

Activity: Make up a movie title. Think in your head what type of movie your title is for (action, scary, funny, etc.). Then write an ad for it. Use words that will make people want to see the movie. In your ad, tell what a person will feel or see when they watch it.

_____

_____

_____

_____

_____

_____

_____

_____

_____

_____

_____

_____

Sound Words

Underline the sentences that help you make a better picture in your head.

1. Carson heard waves.   Carson heard crashing waves.

2. Cassie heard leaves.   Cassie heard leaves rustling.

Writers use sound words like "crash" and "rustle" to help readers sense or feel a place. The words make their writing more interesting. There are lots of sound words. Look at the examples of sound words in the box.

> crash thump bang hiss splash crash knock tap roar ring
> slither pound buzz honk toot buzz hoot bark meow whisper

Activity: Think of a place. It may be a park, a beach, a classroom, a forest, or anywhere you like. Think of all the sounds you might hear. Now, write sentences that describe the place. Use as many sound words as you can.

_____

_____

_____

_____

_____

_____

_____

_____

Lost!

Activity: Write a story with a surprise ending. In your story, write about two people. The people can be you and a friend, or anyone you want. The people are lost. They hear all kinds of jungle animals as they wander around. Describe what the people hear using sound words. For example, the people may hear elephants loudly trumpeting. They may hear hyenas madly laughing. Describe how the people feel when they hear the sounds. Say their hearts pound and thump. Make the reader believe the people are really lost in the jungle.

For your surprise ending, have the people say, "At last! There's the exit of the jungle ride!" or have a teacher say, "This is a great field trip to the zoo!"

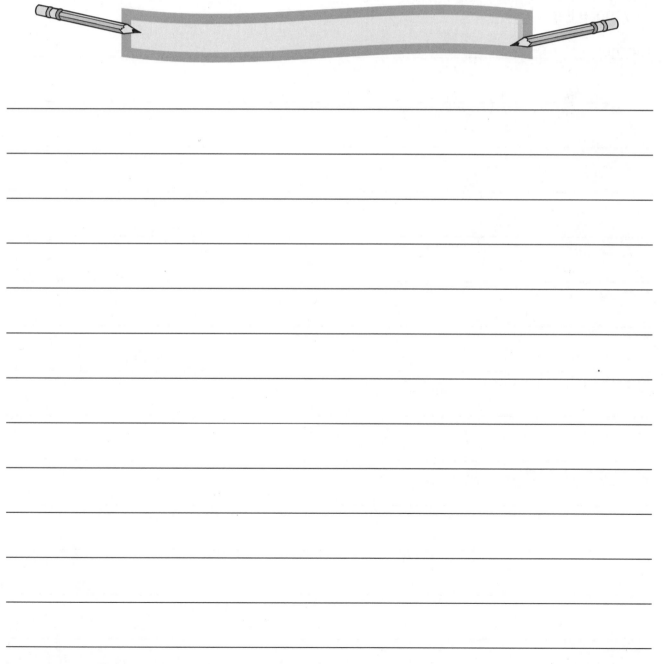

Insect Lesson

Activity: Write a dialogue for a lesson on insects. Have four students each ask the teacher if a scorpion, centipede, worm, and spider are insects. Have the teacher explain that they are not. Use these facts in your answer: Only insects have six legs. Insects have two antennae on their heads. Most adult insects have four wings.

  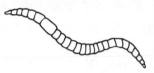 

You can add to your dialogue by having the students tell what the creatures look like or how they make them feel.

Teacher: _____

_____

_____

_____

_____

_____

_____

_____

_____

_____

_____

Bad to Good

THINK ABOUT IT!

Someone calls you an insect. Is that a bad or a good thing? Think about this: Ants are insects. Some ants climb tall trees every day. They carry down leaf bits as heavy as they are. For their size, it is the same as you climbing up Everest and coming down with someone on your back in one day!

Think about this: Grasshoppers are insects. Grasshoppers can jump more than 20 times the length of their bodies. That is the same as you leaping 120 feet in a single bound!

Activity: Write a dialogue between two people. One person wants to hurt the other's feelings. The one person calls the other an insect. How does the second person handle it? He or she thanks the first person! Then he or she tells the first person about ants and grasshoppers. Can you end your dialogue with the first person asking to be friends with the second?

Snake in the River

Which newspaper story would you rather read?

a. "Pet Snake Let Go"

b. "Huge Snake Shocks Swimmers"

Writers choose words for newspaper stories that make people want to read the stories. The word *shocks* sounds like more action than *let go*. The word *huge* sounds more exciting than *pet*.

Activity: Finish writing the newspaper article. In your article, use lots of exciting action words. Make your reader want to keep reading. Use the information in the chart to write your story. Make sure that you include a headline and your byline.

Who	What	When	Where	Why
Dave Neal goes kayaking with friends	spots 11-foot Burmese python	Wildcat Creek, Lafayette, Indiana	August 29, 2010	abandoned or escaped pet because snake can't survive Indiana winters

IMAGINE THAT!

Third Grader Discovers Amazing Treasure

Word Choice

Imagine that you discover or make something. It could be a new invention. It could be a lost treasure. It could be a fossil or a cave. It could be an animal or anything else you want. You choose!

Activity: Write a newspaper article about your find or invention. In your article, tell who, what, where, when, and why. Make people want to read your story by using lots of action words. Make sure that you include a headline and your byline.

HOMES

DID YOU KNOW?

There are five Great Lakes. The names of the lakes are Huron, Ontario, Michigan, Erie, and Superior. It is hard to remember the lake names. Some people have a trick. They use the word HOMES. This is because each lake starts with one of the letters in the word HOMES.

Activity: Write a how-to for memorizing the names of the Great Lakes. Your how-to should have a title. It should have at least six steps.

Extra: What are some animals that make their HOMES in lakes?

_____

_____

_____

_____

_____

_____

_____

_____

_____

_____

_____

_____

_____

No More Pizzas!

When your parents when to school, they may have used this silly, made-up phrase:

My Very Educated Mother Just Served Us Nine Pizzas.

The first letter in each word stood for a planet. The phrase helped one to learn planet order, starting from closest to the Sun. But now there can't be any more pizzas! That's because Pluto is no longer considered a planet! Its classification changed in 2006.

Activity: Make up a new silly phrase to help you remember the planets. Then write a how-to for remembering the planets and their order. Give your how-to a title. Make sure you tell that the order goes from closest to farthest from the Sun.

Mercury   Venus   Earth   Mars   Jupiter   Saturn   Uranus   Neptune

_____

_____

_____

_____

_____

_____

_____

_____

_____

Giraffe Heart

Think of all the words you can that mean the same things as "amazing." Then think of all the words you can that mean the same as "big."

amazing: _____

_____

big: _____

_____

Activity: Now write a paragraph in which you describe a giraffe's heart. When you write, use as many words as you can from your list.

Giraffe Heart Facts

- biggest of land animals
- two feet long
- can weigh 25 pounds
- powerful so it can pump blood up to brain
- special valves in neck arteries so blood doesn't rush to head when giraffe bends down or rush back when giraffe stands

_____

_____

_____

_____

_____

_____

The Face in the Window

DID YOU KNOW?

A giraffe is the tallest land animal. Its neck alone is six feet long and weighs 600 pounds. A giraffe can easily look into a second-story window!

Activity: Write a story in which a giraffe looks into a second-story window. You may use this basic story idea if you want: someone says over and that he or she sees a face in the window. No one believes him or her. Then it turns out that the face belongs to a giraffe.

When you write, use lots of words that help people feel and picture what is going on. Use action words to add excitement.

_____

_____

_____

_____

_____

_____

_____

_____

_____

_____

_____

_____

_____

_____

_____

Like a Tortoise

DID YOU KNOW?

At the age of 61, Cliff Young won a race that no one thought he could win. The race was a running race that was almost 544 miles long! When Young showed up, he was wearing overalls and rubber boots. Young was far behind, but he never stopped—not once! By never sleeping, Young caught up and passed the others. Young was a sheep farmer. He said he was used to running for three days straight on his ranch in Australia when he was rounding up sheep. During the race, Young ran for five days, fifteen hours, and four minutes.

Activity: Write a paragraph in which you compare Young to a tortoise.

Hint: Use the story "The Tortoise and the Hare."

Like a Cheetah

A writer might say someone is like a cheetah. Most likely, the writer would say this to make the reader think the person is:

   a. fast.   or   **b.** slow.

Activity: Make up a person. Tell why the person is like three different things. Each thing can be an animal or an object like a rubber band. Tell why the person is like each thing. Then add a sentence or two that makes a story picture in the reader's head.

Example:

Terry is like a cheetah because she can run fast. One time, Terry missed the school bus. Terry just put her head down and started to run. When the school bus got to the next stop, there was Terry waiting for it!

The Right Name

DID YOU KNOW?

J.K. Rowling wrote all the Harry Potter books. She does not have a middle name. Her first name is Joanne. So why is the author's name on the books "J.K. Rowling"? The publishers wanted to sell the books to boys. They thought boys would not want to read a book by a woman and said, "Two initials will be better." Rowling chose the K because she had a grandmother whose name started with K.

Activity: Give your opinion: Does a book author's name matter? Do you think Rowling sold more books with the initials J.K.? Do you think boys only want books by men? Do you think girls only want books by women? What you write cannot be wrong because it is what you think. Use your own experiences for examples.

_____

_____

_____

_____

_____

_____

_____

_____

_____

Boy or Girl?

Activity: Think of two initials to be the name of a person. Now write a short tale about this person. In your story, tell of a time when people find out that the person they thought was a boy or a girl isn't!

_____

_____

_____

_____

_____

_____

_____

_____

_____

_____

_____

_____

_____

Hippo Keeper's Log

DID YOU KNOW?

Owen was a baby hippo. He was abandoned by his mother and badly in need of water. Luckily, Owen was found. On December 27, 2004, Owen was taken to Haller Park in Kenya. There, something new and unexpected happened. Owen became friends with a giant tortoise! The tortoise was over 100 years old. Its name was Mzee. Owen would lick Mzee's face and sleep with his head on Mzee.

Activity: Write an entry in a log Owen's keeper might have kept when Owen first arrived. A log is like a diary. It tells when and what happens. Include your thoughts and feelings in the log, too.

Time writing

Put a colon (:) between the hour and the minute.

Use AM or a.m. for before noon.

Use PM or p.m. for afternoon.

Date: _____   Location: _____

Time: _____

_____

_____

_____

_____

_____

_____

_____

_____

Pet Journal

IMAGINE THAT!

Imagine that you can have a pet. The pet can be any kind of animal. Your pet can be wild, big, small, loud, or cute.

Activity: Write a journal entry about your pet. You can write about when your pet first comes to live with you. Tell what it looks like and how you feel. Write about what you do with your pet, what you teach your pet, or how you care for it. You can write about something your pet did or how people act when they see your pet. It is up to you!

Date: _____   Location: _____

Time: _____

_____

_____

_____

_____

_____

_____

_____

_____

_____

_____

_____

_____

_____

Action!

Which sentences sound as if there is more action?

a. Emma **swam** to the shore when she saw the shark fin.

b. Emma **raced** to the shore when she saw the shark fin.

a. Eddie **looked** at the crocodile that **got** on the bus.

b. Eddie **stared** at the crocodile that **crawled** on the bus.

When you write, you can use action words to help keep your reader interested.

Activity: Write a letter to a friend or relative in which you use lots of action words. In your letter, tell about a time you **raced** instead of walked or swam, **guzzled** instead of drank, or **pounded** instead of knocked.

Dear _____ ,

_____

_____

_____

_____

_____

_____

_____

Your friend, niece/nephew, cousin, granddaughter/son,

_____

Plane Down!

What sentences sound as if there is more action?

a. Libby **got** up out of her chair.

b. Libby **leaped** up out of her chair.

a. Luke **took** a breath of air.

b. Luke **gasped** for air.

When you write, you can use action words to help keep your reader interested.

Activity: Imagine that your plane goes down. Fortunately, you have a parachute. Where do you land? What do you see? What happens? It is up to you. Wherever you are, exciting things happen to you.

After you are saved or save yourself, you write a letter to a friend. Fill your letter with action words when you say what happened to you and what you did.

Dear _____ ,

You would not believe _____

_____

_____

_____

_____

_____

_____

_____

_____

Mystery Item

DID YOU KNOW? An adjective is a kind of word that describes or tells about a noun. (A noun is a person, place, thing, or idea.) An adjective might tell the color or size of something, or how something feels, tastes, or smells.

What words could be adjectives? Circle the six adjectives.

small   angry   chair   seven   hard   finger   sweet   loud

Now it's your turn to think of adjectives. Think of five adjectives you could use to describe a:

cat: _____

_____

mouse: _____

_____

hat: _____

_____

Activity: Think of an item. Your item could be a person, animal, or thing. Write several sentences about your item. Write about how it looks, what it does, where it lives, and how it acts. Use lots of adjectives, but do not ever say what your item is! Instead, write what your item is on the back of the page. Let people read your sentences, or read them out loud. Can anyone figure out what your mystery item is?

_____

_____

_____

_____

_____

_____

The Dove and the Ant

DID YOU KNOW? Aesop lived long ago. Aesop was a Greek storyteller. He told fables. Fables are short stories with a moral. A moral is like a lesson.

Activity: Look at the bare facts of "The Dove and the Ant," one of Aesop's stories. Rewrite the story. When you write, use lots of adjectives and action words. Describe how the ant and the dove feel. Make it so the reader can picture what is going on and doesn't want to stop reading.

At the end, write a one-sentence moral. It should be a lesson about the size of friends.

1. The ant falls in river when it goes to drink.

2. The dove feels sorry for and it throws in a branch.

3. The ant gets to shore on the branch.

4. Later, the ant sees the man aiming a gun at the dove.

5. The ant bites the man's foot.

6. The man misses the dove.

_____

_____

_____

_____

_____

_____

_____

Metaphor Poem

How do you make a metaphor? Take two nouns. (A noun is a person, place, thing, or idea.) Compare or contrast the nouns to one another.

Writers use metaphors to help readers make pictures in their minds or to feel a certain way. For example, if I say, I am a rainbow, do you get the feeling I am:

a. unhappy and dull? or **b.** bright and happy?

Activity: Write a metaphor poem. Compare or contrast yourself to something else. You can compare yourself to a book, a river, an apple, a bird, a song, or a ball. You can be whatever you want! Your poem should have a minimum of five lines. It can be as long as you want.

Start your poem, *I am a* _____ .

> I am a rainbow
> adding color to the world.
> My bright smile stops
> my sister's tears.
> I am a rainbow
> reaching across the sky
> to find a pot of gold
> of my own making.

_____

_____

_____

_____

_____

_____

Fluency

The Dodo

DID YOU KNOW?

A dodo was a large bird that couldn't fly. It weighed about **44** pounds. It lived on an island in the Indian Ocean. There are no dodos alive today. They are extinct because sailors who sailed to the island ate them. The last dodo was killed in the **17**th century.

You can make up a rhyme about a dodo. Rhymes can make reading fun. When you read or say rhymes out loud, the words seem to flow. They make a pattern that is easy to listen to or say.

You will never see a dodo with a pink and purple yoyo.

Activity: Make up other rhymes about animals. The animals can be living or extinct. Start your rhymes with all or any of these starts:

> • You will never see
> • I hope to see
> • It would by funny to see
> • How strange to see

_____

_____

_____

_____

_____

_____

_____

Seeing a Dodo

Activity: Write a dialogue with rhymes between two people. The rhymes will make your dialogue fun to say.

Make up names for the people. Have one person keep telling the other all the crazy or strange animals he or she sees. Have the second person say it can't be true. Find out at the end that the person saw the strange things in a book, circus, party, parade, or movie.

Example:

Ben: Today I saw a dodo with a pink and purple yoyo.

Benita: You couldn't have seen a dodo with a pink and purple yoyo! That's as silly as seeing a cat with an umbrella and a hat!

Super Bats

DID YOU KNOW?

Bats are mammals. They are the only mammals that can fly. There are nearly 1,000 kinds of bats. Baby bats drink milk. Most bats eat insects, and that helps keep pests from biting us or hurting our crops. Other bats eat fruit or fish. Bats sleep by hanging from their feet. The biggest bat weighs about two pounds and has a wingspan of six feet! The smallest bat weighs less than a penny! It is the size of a bumblebee.

How do you feel about bats? Some people do not like them. Other people find them really interesting. Write down all the words one might use to describe bats and how he or she feels about them.

likes bats	does not like bats
super	scary

Activity: Write a short paragraph in which you tell how you feel about bats and why. Include some bat facts in your paragraph.

_____

_____

_____

_____

_____

_____

_____

Vampire Bats

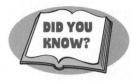

DID YOU KNOW?

Very few bats drink blood. These bats are known as vampire bats. Vampire bats hunt only when it is dark. They creep up to large sleeping animals. Then they make a small cut with their teeth and lap up some blood. Usually the animal never knows it was a meal!

Vampire bats take care of each other. A motherless bat will be taken care of. Vampire bats need to eat every two days. If one can't find food, other bats will spit up some blood for it.

Activity: Imagine that your uncle sent you a gift box. Inside the box you find seven vampire bats! Is this a good gift or a not-so-good gift? Write a paragraph in which you tell why. Include some vampire bat facts in your paragraph.

Remember—there is no right or wrong answer. You are the writer, so you can decide.

_____

_____

_____

_____

_____

_____

_____

_____

_____

The Garden

When you write, you need to make sure your story makes sense. Why doesn't the story below make sense? (*Hint:* two things don't make sense)

When I was little, I planted a garden. First, I went to the store and bought carrot, lettuce, and radish seeds. I also bought some tomato seedlings. Then I went behind my house. I dug up the ground and planted the seeds. I transplanted the seedlings. That night I ate all the carrots, lettuce, potatoes, and tomatoes that I had grown.

In the story, it sounds as if it only took one day for all the things to grow! Also, the reader does not know for sure that the writer planted potatoes.

How could you fix this story so it makes sense?

1. _____

2. _____

Activity: Write about true things that you did one summer or winter, or on a windy or rainy day. Include something in your story that does not make sense. For example, you might tell what you do in the winter, but in your story you describe a hot summer day! Show or read your paragraph to your classmates. Could anyone tell what didn't make sense?

_____

_____

_____

_____

_____

_____

_____

The Octopus

When you write, you need to make sure your story makes sense. Why doesn't the story below make sense? (*Hint:* two things don't make sense.)

> *I wanted to see an octopus. I put on my bathing suit, held my breath, and dove down, deep under the water. After ten minutes, I reached the bottom of the ocean. There was a rock half in and half out of the water. An octopus was sitting on the rock!*

How can one hold his or her breath for ten minutes? How can a rock be half in and half out of the water if it is at the bottom of the ocean?

How could you fix this story so it makes sense?

1. _____

2. _____

Activity: Make up a story in which at least one thing does not make sense. Your story can be about going somewhere or doing something. It can be about anything you want. Show or read your story to your classmates. Could anyone tell what didn't make sense?

_____

_____

_____

_____

_____

_____

_____

_____

Mood Poems

Rewrite the lines under the feelings they go with.

> Hurting because of my lost pet
> Days the sun shines brightly
> An unexpected present in the mail
> Dark clouds covering the sky
> A smile from a stranger
> Salty tears running down my face

Happiness

1. _____

2. _____

3. _____

Sadness

1. _____

2. _____

3. _____

Writers choose words to match the mood of the piece they are writing. "Happy," "smile," and "brightly" go together. "Dark" and "hurt" do not go with "happy." The words help the reader feel what the writer wants them to.

Activity: Write two mood poems. One should be about how you feel when you are happy and/or things that make you happy, the other about how you feel when you are sad and/or things that make you sad. Each poem should be at least seven lines long.

_____   _____

_____   _____

_____   _____

_____   _____

_____   _____

Night for the Fox

DID YOU KNOW?

For you, night is a time to sleep and rest. Is it for a fennec fox? The fennec fox is the smallest fox. It lives in the hot Sahara desert of North Africa. To escape the heat, it is nocturnal. When something is nocturnal, it is mostly active at night. The fennec fox has huge eyes and ears. It has hair on the bottom of its feet to protect it from the hot sand. The fennec fox is an omnivore. This means it eats both meat and plants. It may eat insects, lizards, snails, birds, eggs, and fruit.

Activity: Imagine you are a fennec fox. Write a poem about the night. Use words that fit how the fox feels about the night. Can you include some facts about the fennec fox in your poem?

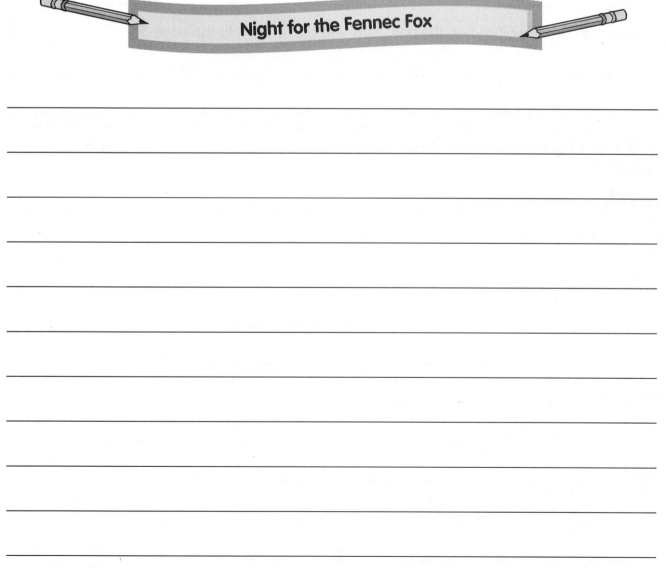

Night for the Fennec Fox

_____

_____

_____

_____

_____

_____

_____

_____

_____

_____

59

The Gorilla

When you write, you do not want all your sentences to look the same. You want some long ones, and you want some short ones. This keeps your writing interesting.

Make short sentences long by following this example:

Binti Jua is a gorilla. Binti Jua lives in a zoo in Chicago, Illinois.

Binti Jua is a gorilla **that** lives in a zoo in Chicago, Illinois.

Your turn:

One day, Binti Jua saved a three-year-old boy. The boy had climbed a wall and had fallen 18 feet down onto concrete.

_____ who _____

_____

Binti Jua carefully picked up the boy. Binti Jua carried him to the cage door.

_____ and _____

_____

Activity: Now write two short sentences of your own. Then turn them into one long sentence.

Short: **1.** _____

2. _____

Long: _____

_____

_____

Short: **1.** _____

2. _____

Long: _____

_____

Gorilla News

Activity: Imagine that you are a reporter. You are telling the story of Binti Jua, the gorilla. Write down what you will say. Make some of your sentences long and others short. This makes the news easier to listen to. It helps people pay attention. Say your newscast out loud. Did the difference in sentence length improve the newscast?

Facts
- August 16, 1996
- Chicago, Illinois
- three-year-old boy climbed wall, fell 18 feet onto concrete
- Binti Jua climbed down, carefully picked up boy
- growled at big gorilla that came close
- patted boy on back
- carried 60 feet to door; waited for keepers
- boy in hospital for four days

Good morning, listeners. This is _____.

_____

_____

_____

_____

_____

_____

_____

_____

_____

Stop, Drop, and Hold On!

THINK ABOUT IT!

Sometimes, it is easier to learn things when they are in a list. What if you needed to teach people what to do in case of an earthquake?

Activity: Write down what to do in list/poster form. This will make it easier for people to remember. First, make a title for your poster. Your title should tell what your instructions are for. Have three sections. The sections should be indoors, outdoors, and moving vehicle. Number the directions in each section. You decide how many steps to include.

Use the following information for your steps:

> If you are indoors, drop to the ground. Take cover by getting under a table or desk. Hold on until the shaking stops. If there is nothing to get under, cover your face and head with your arms. Then crouch in an inside corner of the building. Stay away from glass and windows. Stay inside until the shaking stops. Don't use elevators.
>
> If you are outdoors, stay there. Move away from buildings and wires. If you are in a moving vehicle, stop when it is safe and stay inside. Try to stay away from buildings, wires, or bridges.

_____

_____

_____

_____

_____

_____

_____

_____

What was easier to read: your list/poster, or all the information above?

Earthquake!

Activity: Imagine that you are at school, and there is an earthquake. Describe what you do and how you feel. Make your writing exciting to read. Use words that help the reader feel what you or other students feel.

Here I Sit!

Where do you sit in your classroom? You can say where things are using different words. Using different words helps keep your writing from being the same. It helps your reader stay interested.

Activity: Write down five sentences describing where you sit.

In sentence:

1—say who or what is in **front** of you.

2—say who or what is **behind** you.

3—say who or what is to the **left** of you.

4—say who or what is to the **right** of you.

5—say if you are in the **front half** or **back half** of the room.

6—say if you are in the **middle**, **left**, or **right side** of the room.

7—put the information from at least two sentences into one long sentence.

Examples for 7:

I sit in the front half of the room on the right-hand side.

Julianne and Mark sit in front of me, and Maya and Jorge sit in back of me.

Dinner Party at the Farm

Fluency

IMAGINE THAT!

Imagine you are having a dinner party at a farm. You will be there with four animal guests. Decide what four animals you will invite. Write down where you and the animals will sit.

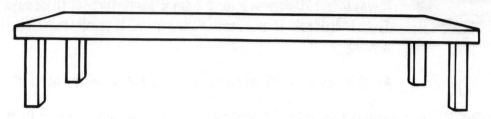

Activity: Write down five sentences describing where you are and where your guests sit. In sentence:

1—say who is at the head of the table.

2—say who is directly across from the head at the other end.

3—say who is sitting to the left of the head.

4—say who is sitting to the right of the head.

5—say who is sitting at the table going clockwise from the head.

6—put the information from at least two sentences into one long sentence.

Examples for 6:

I will sit at the head of the table, and the cow will sit directly across from me at the other end.

I will sit at the end, with the donkey to my right and the dog to my left.

_____

_____

_____

_____

_____

_____

Death Valley

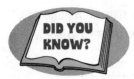

DID YOU KNOW?

Death Valley is the hottest, driest, and lowest place in the United States. It had the hottest day ever recorded in the United States; it was 134 degrees F! One summer it was over 120 degrees F for 52 days! Forty-three of those days were all in a row! There is little rain to cool Death Valley down. It usually rains less than two inches a year.

Death Valley is a national park. It has over three million acres of wilderness.

Activity: Write a want ad for a Death Valley park ranger. Use words that make the ranger want to work there. Think of ways to make the heat and the dryness sound great!

Pecos Bill

Pecos Bill was a cowboy who could ride anything. Once it had not rained for a long time. The land was dry and dusty, and nothing could grow. So Pecos Bill jumped on a tornado! The tornado whipped and lashed and spun around. Pecos Bill wouldn't let go. He just squeezed out water for the dry land below. When Pecos Bill fell off, he landed in California. He made such a deep hole when he fell that he made Death Valley.

This story is an American folk tale. The story is made up, but Death Valley is real.

Activity: Now it is your turn to make up a story about Pecos Bill. Plan ahead. Choose a real thing Pecos Bill can make. It can be a mountain, lake, canyon, ocean, river, or anything you want. Explain how it was made because of Pecos Bill. Did he cough, dig, cry, or lasso something? You decide! Make your story fun to listen to.

Plan Ahead:

What he made	What he did to make it

_____

_____

_____

_____

_____

_____

_____

Head to Toe

THINK ABOUT IT!

What if you were teaching a baby about body parts? Start at the baby's head. Then "walk" over the baby's body with your fingers, always keeping at least one finger on the baby. This means you cannot go from a hand to a foot. You can only go from a hand to a wrist. Go up and down at least one arm and leg. Say the name of each part when you get to it.

Activity: Write down what you would say to the baby. Make long and short sentences that are fun to say. Try to use these words at least once: **now**, **next**, **after**, **below**, **up**, **down**

Start your lesson like this:

Baby, baby, do you feel me touching your head? Now I'm . . .

_____

_____

_____

_____

_____

_____

_____

_____

_____

_____

_____

What Was I Petting?

IMAGINE THAT!

Imagine that it is very dark. You stumble into an animal. You think it is your cat or dog, so you pick it up and start to pet it.

Activity: Write down the thoughts that go through your head as you pet your animal. In your thoughts, you should say what part of the animal you are feeling. You may wonder why some parts are missing, or worry when you feel some things you do not expect. Then the light comes on, and you find out that you are holding a _____!

You will have to plan ahead for this story. Before you start writing, think of an animal that feels a bit different from a cat or a dog. This story is made up, so the animal can be anything you want.

_____

_____

_____

_____

_____

_____

_____

_____

_____

_____

_____

On This Date

On February 20, 1947, fruit flies were sent into space.
Fruit flies were sent into space on February 20, 1947.

What is different about these sentences? _____

A man walked on the moon for the first time on July 20, 1969.
On July 20, 1969, a man walked on the moon for the first time.

What is different about these sentences? _____

A writer can make sentences in different ways. This keeps the writing interesting. What sounds best? It depends. A writer just has to read what he or she has written and pick what sounds best. A writer wants sentences that sound natural and flow together.

Activity: Write three sentences about the day you were born.

1. On _____ , I was born in _____.
              date   where

2. I was born on _____ _____.
                          date   where

3. _____ I was born on _____.
            where   date

Circle the sentence you like best. Now write two more sentences about yourself.

_____

_____

_____

_____

_____

_____

What's on Top?

Underline these words in each pairs of sentences: **on top of the**

> There is a man on top of the horse.
> On top of the man there is a dog.

> There is a cat on top of the dog.
> On top of the cat there is a mouse.

You can put **on top of the** at the front or end of a sentence.

Activity: Now it is your turn to make sentences like the ones above.

First, think of seven animals or things that go from large to smaller.

Then, write sentences like the ones above, mixing up where you put **on top of the** _____.

You may end your story with your own or these words: *What's on top? Nothing is on top! They all fell down!*

Read your story out loud. Was it fun to read?

_____

_____

_____

_____

_____

_____

_____

_____

Thank-You Letter

Activity: Sending a thank-you note is good manners. Write a thank-you letter to someone you know. The thank-you can be for a gift or time spent with you.

Follow these easy steps when you write your letter:

1. Greet the person properly. (Dear Mr., Mrs., or first name if they are your age or a friend)
2. Thank them for the gift. (*Example:* Thank you so much for the silk parachute.)
3. Write one or two sentences about what you did with the gift, why you like it, or what you plan to do with it. (*Example:* I plan on jumping out of an airplane on Tuesday, and the parachute will be very helpful.)
4. Tell the giver they were nice to think of you. (*Example:* It was nice of you to take time out of your busy day to come to our class.)
5. If you can, mention something about the giver. (*Example:* I hope your pet turtle gets better soon.)
6. End your letter with *Love, Warm Regards, Sincerely,* or *Yours Truly.*

_____

_____

_____

_____

_____

_____

_____

_____

_____

What a Gift!

Activity: Imagine that you are sent a gift. The gift can be from a made-up person or a real person. The gift can be anything you want! It can be a superpower, a trip around the world, or a strange or unusual pet. Use your imagination. Write a thank-you note for the gift using the steps listed below. Have fun in Step 3 in which you talk about what you did with your gift!

1. Greet the person properly. (Dear Mr., Mrs., or first name if they are your age or a friend)

2. Thank them for the gift. (*Example:* Thank you so much for the silk parachute.)

3. Write one or two sentences about what you did with the gift, why you like it, or what you plan to do with it. (*Example:* I plan on jumping out of an airplane on Tuesday, and the parachute will be very helpful.)

4. Tell the giver they were nice to think of you. (*Example:* It was nice of you to take time out of your busy day to come to our class.)

5. If you can, mention something about the giver. (*Example:* I hope your pet turtle gets better soon.)

6. End your letter with *Love*, *Warm Regards*, *Sincerely*, or *Yours Truly*.

_____

_____

_____

_____

_____

_____

_____

_____

Travel Writer

DID YOU KNOW?

Some writers are travel writers. Travel writers write about places they visit or things that happen in faraway places. They talk about where they stayed, what they saw, what they ate, and what they did. They talk about things they could have done, too.

Activity: Think of a place you have gone. It can be a faraway or nearby place. Write an article about it. It is your trip that you are writing about, so you can use the word **I** in your article. You can write as if you are still in the place, or you have just come back. Make sure you include a title for your article and your byline.

In your article:

- tell what and where the place is

- tell how you got there

- tell where you stayed or can stay

- tell what you did or can do, see, buy, or eat there

- advise when the best time is to go and who should go

Title _____

Byline _____

_____

_____

_____

_____

_____

_____

_____

Warm-Up

Ice Hotel

Fluency

74

 **DID YOU KNOW?**

There is a hotel in Norway that you can't stay in every year. That is because it melts! Then, every year, it is rebuilt. The hotel is at the edge of the Arctic Circle. It is built every January. It melts every spring. The hotel has 30 bedrooms. It has rooms to meet and talk. Everything in the hotel is made of ice—the beds, chairs, tables, and even the cups! The hotel provides warm sleeping bags.

People who go to the Ice Hotel hope to see the Northern Lights. Many people take trips on snowmobiles or ride a sled driven by reindeer.

Activity: Imagine you are a travel writer who has gone to the Ice Hotel. Write a story about your stay there. Give facts about the hotel, but also tell what you feel and like. Make sure you include a title for your article and your byline.

Title _____

Byline _____

_____

_____

_____

_____

_____

_____

_____

_____

Tongue Twisters

DID YOU KNOW?

Tongue twisters are fun, but they are very hard to say. Tongue twisters have repeating sounds which can be at the start or the end of the words.

Read the tongue twisters. Can you say them quickly? *Warning:* They are harder to say than they look!

(*Note:* A tutor is a teacher. When you tutor someone, you teach them.)

A tutor who tooted a flute
Tried to tutor two tooters to toot.
Said the two to the tutor,
"Is it harder to toot
Or to tutor two tooters to toot?"

She sells seashells on the seashore.

Activity: Now write your own tongue twisters.

1. Use some of these words: big, black, bug, bear, beetle, bit, but

2. Use words that rhyme or mostly start with any letter but "b."

3. Use words that rhyme or mostly start with different letters than the letters used in your other tongue twisters.

_____

_____

_____

_____

_____

_____

_____

Voice

Open and Close

Voice

THINK ABOUT IT!

A law is a rule. People make and pass laws. Sometimes states and cities have old laws that are no longer needed, or do not make sense. Some of these old laws are still there because it would take time and work to remove them. One state had a law about gates. It was a crime to open a gate and then fail to close it!

Activity: Think about this law. Then write a few sentences in which you:

- tell why you think this law was made.

- explain where this law might make sense.

- describe a time when it was important that you close a gate.

- say if you think we need this law today.

_____

_____

_____

_____

_____

_____

_____

_____

_____

_____

_____

_____

The 50-Pound Box of Candy

Voice

IMAGINE THAT! A rumor is a story that is told as true but it may or may not be true. People like to write about a law in Idaho. Most likely, this law is not true. What do people say the law says? They say that in Idaho it is against the law for one person to give another person a box of candy that weighs more than 50 pounds!

Activity: Imagine that this law is real. Imagine it is against the law to give a person a box of candy that weighs more than 50 pounds. Write a story in which you tell why this law was made. You can make your story sound true or untrue. It is up to you.

_____

_____

_____

_____

_____

_____

_____

_____

_____

_____

_____

_____

The Best Boarding

Voice

THINK ABOUT IT! Think of Hawaii. Think of riding a board. Most likely, you thought of surfboarding. People do not think of snowboarding, but you can snowboard in Hawaii! In fact, you can snowboard and surfboard on the same day!

Mauna Kea is on the Big Island. It is 13,500 feet high, and in the winter months, it is covered with snow. There are no ski lifts. At the top, you have a view in every direction. You can see the ocean.

Activity: Is it better to snowboard or surfboard in Hawaii? There is no right or wrong answer. Think about what you like. Then explain what you would do. Give reasons why.

Board Advice

Activity: Imagine that three aliens come to visit you. Alien 1 tells you it is going to visit Kansas. Alien 2 tells you it is going to visit California. Alien 3 tells you it is going to visit Colorado. Between the three aliens, they have one snowboard, one surfboard, and one skateboard. The Aliens ask you for advice. They want to know what board each one should take. Write down your advice. Tell the aliens your reasons why.

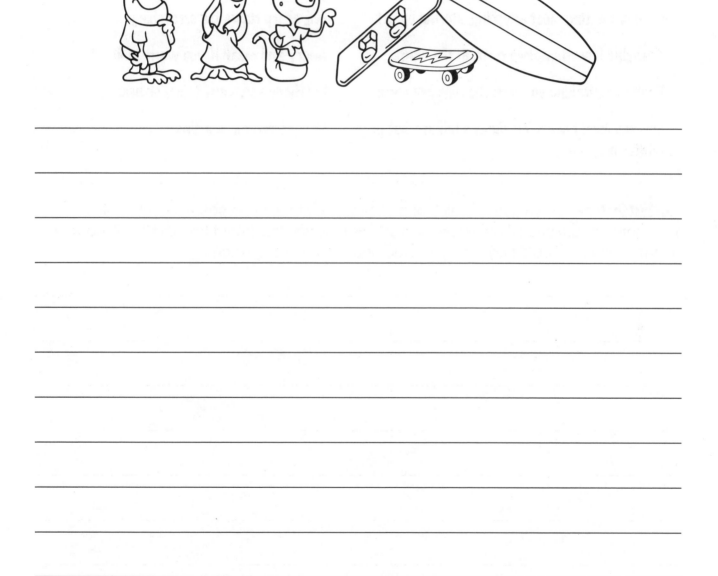

_____

_____

_____

_____

_____

_____

_____

_____

_____

_____

_____

_____

_____

Bears

Voice

THINK ABOUT IT! Think about bears. Some people like them. They think they are interesting and like to look at them. They would like to study them. Other people do not like bears and are afraid of them. Look at the two name poems. In each poem, the first letter of each line spells out the name "bears." Which writer likes bears best?

Beautiful brown bears.	Beastly brown bears.
Each one eating most anything, storing up fat.	Evil, sharp claws for scratching.
Amazing how they sleep through the winter.	Angry and mean if you want to fish, too.
Really not waking up when the cubs are born!	Rarely do you want to see or hear one.
Summer heart beats 70 times a minute, but in winter only 10.	Sharp teeth for snarling.

Activity: Now it is your turn. Think of an animal. Write a name poem for your animal. Your name poem should be written so it shows how you feel about the animal. Read your poem to others. Could they tell if you liked or didn't like the animal?

_____

_____

_____

_____

_____

_____

_____

_____

_____

The Opposite

Activity: On a previous day, you wrote a name poem about an animal. You wrote about the animal in a way that showed how you feel about the animal. You used words that sounded good or not so good. Today you have to imagine you feel the opposite!

Did you use words that made the animal seem scary or creepy? Today you have to use words that make it sound great! Did you use words that made an animal seem great? Today you have to make it seem the opposite!

Writing this poem does not mean you have changed your mind or how you feel. Today you are just writing from a different viewpoint.

_____

_____

_____

_____

_____

_____

_____

_____

Was it hard to write from a different viewpoint?   _____ yes   _____ no

The Dog and the Wolf

Read Aesop's tale of "The Dog and the Wolf" below. Aesop was a storyteller from long ago. Aesop's stories were written to teach people lessons.

A skinny wolf was almost dead from hunger. A fat dog came upon the wolf. The fat dog said, "Brother, your life will be the end of you. Come do a steady job as I do. You will get food every day."

This sounded good to the wolf, so he went with the dog. The wolf saw that the hair on the dog's neck had worn away. The dog told him his master put a collar on him every night and chained him up. "It rubs a bit," said the dog, "but you get used to it."

That's when the wolf said, "Good-bye!"

Activity: Write down your thoughts about this story. When you write, tell:

- if the dog or the wolf had the better life and why.

- what you think the lesson was.

- if the story was worth reading.

Remember, what you write cannot be wrong. It is your view. It is your opinion.

_____

_____

_____

_____

_____

_____

_____

Inside the Dog or Wolf's Head

You may have read this story about the dog and wolf before. Here it is again.

A skinny wolf was almost dead from hunger. A fat dog came upon the wolf. The fat dog said, "Brother, your life will be the end of you. Come do a steady job as I do. You will get food every day."

This sounded good to the wolf, so he went with the dog. The wolf saw that the hair on the dog's neck had worn away. The dog told him his master put a collar on him every night and chained him up. "It rubs a bit," said the dog, "but you get used to it."

That's when the wolf said, "Good-bye!"

Activity: Rewrite the story from a different viewpoint. You can be the dog or the wolf. Write down all the thoughts that go through your head when you see the other animal, and what you think when the story ends. Did you feel sorry for the other animal? When you write, use the word **I**. That is because in the story, you are the dog or the wolf.

_____

_____

_____

_____

_____

_____

_____

_____

_____

The Bridge Painter

DID YOU KNOW?

The San Francisco Golden Gate Bridge is painted orange. The bridge is being painted all the time. There are **38** painters. The painters do not start at one end and go to the other. They touch up places where it is needed. The painters have to battle wind, sea air, and fog. They have to work in the cold and the heat. They have to work high up in the air.

Activity: What do you think it looks like when a bridge painter looks down? Write a dialogue in which you interview a bridge painter. Ask him what cars, boats, and people are like when he looks down. Answer how you think they look. You can ask other questions, too.

What Color?

THINK ABOUT IT! The color of the Golden Gate Bridge is not carbon black. It is not steel gray. It is "International Orange." Why is the bridge this color? People felt it blended into the natural setting. Also, it was a color very different from the sky and the sea. This makes it easy for sailors to spot.

Activity: Write a dialogue. Make up names for the two people who are talking. Then have them talk about a new color for the bridge. Have the people say why the colors are good or bad. Make names for the colors (**example:** carbon black and steel gray). Your dialogue can be silly or serious.

_____

_____

_____

_____

_____

_____

_____

_____

_____

_____

Letter to the President

Voice

DID YOU KNOW?

Abraham Lincoln was running for president. He did not have a beard. Then he got a letter from Grace Bedell, an eleven-year-old girl. Grace told Lincoln that if he had a beard, "you would look a great deal better for your face is so thin." Lincoln did grow a beard! Then he was elected president. He was the 16th president.

Activity: Write your own letter to the president. You can tell the president anything you want. You can tell him how he should spend money, what he should do, or how he should eat or dress.

This kind of letter is a formal letter. It is not the kind of letter you write to your friends.

For this type of letter, you include your school address, the president's address, and the date. You address the president as Mr. or Ms. President. You end the letter with "Sincerely" and then your first and last name.

The White House
1600 Pennsylvania Avenue NW
Washington, DC 20500

School address: _____

_____

_____
    date

Dear _____ :

_____

_____

_____

_____

_____

_____

_____,

_____

First and last name

Silly Riddles

Activity: Imagine that you have a friend who loves riddles or jokes. Whenever you hear a new riddle or joke, you send it to your friend. Write a letter with some riddles or jokes that you like. You can use your own riddles or jokes, or you can use the riddles on this page.

A letter to a friend is not a formal letter. It can be silly. You can sign your name any way you like.

When is a black dog most likely to go into a white house?

When the door is open!

What kind of coat goes on wet and has no buttons?

A coat of paint!

What kind of a dog can jump higher than a building?

Any dog! Buildings can't jump!

_____

_____

_____

_____

_____

_____

_____

_____

The Date Line

Voice

DID YOU KNOW?

There is a line for adding and subtracting days. What kind of line is this? It is the International Date Line. What happens if you cross this line going east? You subtract a day, or 24 hours! This means you could have two birthdays! What happens if you cross this line going west? You add a day! This means that the date is the eastern-side date plus one calendar day.

Activity: Write two journal entries. Each journal entry should have the same date as your birthday. Explain in your journal why you can have two birthdays. Tell how you crossed the International Date Line (plane or boat). Tell what you might have done to celebrate your birthday.

Australia Diary

Activity: Imagine that you crossed the International Date Line and went to Australia. You kept a diary. In it, you told what you did or saw. Make at least two entries in your diary. Use what you know about Australia. Use some of the words Australians use, too.

Australian English		American English
tin	=	can
station	=	ranch
jackaroo	=	cowboy
jillaroo	=	cowgirl
queue	=	line
lift	=	elevator
ute	=	pickup truck
flat	=	apartment

Australia

_____   _____

_____   _____

_____   _____

_____   _____

_____   _____

_____   _____

_____   _____

_____   _____

_____   _____

Safety Talk

Voice

Activity: You are giving a how-to talk to kindergartners. Your talk is on how to stay safe on a bike. Write down what you will tell the children. Break it down into short rules and reasons why so they will remember.

Before you write, think about:

- helmets
- wearing brightly colored clothes
- direction (ride with traffic, walk against)

- riding in single file
- traffic signs and lights
- where to cross, and looking left-right-left

The Right Way

IMAGINE THAT!

Imagine you have a visitor from Australia. You take your visitor for a walk. The visitor wants to walk on the right side of the road. You say you have to walk on the left. Explain that it is the safest side for walking. The safest side is when you walk against the traffic. Explain that bikes are different. Bikes go with traffic on the right side.

You get into a big argument! Is it the right side or the left side? Then have a car pass by. Have the visitor say that the car is on the wrong side of the road. That is when you both realize that cars in Australia and the U.S. drive on opposite sides of the road!

Activity: Write a dialog that takes place on this walk.

_____

_____

_____

_____

_____

_____

_____

_____

_____

_____

_____

_____

Tears of Laughter

THINK ABOUT IT!

Have you heard someone say, "I laughed until I cried"? How about, "I laughed so hard the tears were running down my face!"?

Activity: Think of a time that you laughed and laughed, or you made someone else laugh. Write about what made you laugh or how you made someone laugh. Was it a joke? Was it a scene in a movie? Was it a trick? Was it someone tickling you? What made you laugh and laugh?

Give details about where, when, why, and what.

* Some people laugh when they are nervous or afraid. If you want, you can tell about a time when you gave a nervous laugh.

_____

_____

_____

_____

_____

_____

_____

_____

_____

_____

_____

The Funny Dog

Activity: Write a story that includes a funny dog as the main character. A person or people think the dog is funny because it laughs and laughs. At the end of the story, have people find out that the dog is not a funny dog. It is a spotted hyena!

_____

_____

_____

_____

_____

_____

_____

_____

_____

_____

_____

_____

_____

_____

The Penny

THINK ABOUT IT!

When you think of a penny, do you think of something:

a. worth a lot?   or   b. worth a little?

Activity: Describe a penny.

When you write, tell:

- its color, size, shape, and weight.

- if you can buy anything with it.

- if it would make you feel rich.

- how some people want to do away with pennies. They say prices should end with the numbers 0 or 5 (**Example:** $1.00 or $1.05). Tell if you agree or disagree. Give at least one reason why.

_____

_____

_____

_____

_____

_____

_____

_____

_____

Finding Treasure

Activity: Imagine you are in the future. Write a story in which you go on a treasure hunt. When you write, use the word **I**. This is because you will be narrating the story. You will tell what you see and what you do. You will be describing things. Then, tell where you are and how you feel when you find the treasure.

What is the treasure? It is twenty pennies from long ago! Tell how the pennies are worth a lot of money because they are so rare! Tell how long ago people used to use them to buy things, and what you think about that. Then tell what you will do with your treasure. Will you sell it for lots of money, or will you keep it?

_____

_____

_____

_____

_____

_____

_____

_____

_____

_____

_____

Game Action!

Activity: Think of a game or physical activity you participated in. It could be soccer, baseball, jumping rope—anything you want. Then, describe the action. Tell what is going on from your point of view. Use the word **I**.

Example: I grabbed the bat. Taking a deep breath, I stepped up to the plate. I saw the ball coming close, close, closer!

_____

_____

_____

_____

_____

_____

_____

_____

_____

_____

_____

Bat, Ball, or Rope

Activity: Previously, you wrote about a game or physical activity. You wrote from your own point of view. Today you are going to write about the same game or activity. Only this time, you are going to write from a different point of view! You will be something that was used in the game. It could be a ball, bat, rope, or even your shoe! You will write as if you are the thing you choose. The thing telling the story will write from the **I** point of view.

Example: Oh no, here we go again. This sweaty, dirty hand is coming toward me. Is it going to pick me up? Yes, I'm being picked up. Now I'm being swung around! I hope I don't get dizzy!

_____

_____

_____

_____

_____

_____

_____

_____

_____

_____

_____

The Best Tree

Activity: Write a paragraph about how you feel about trees. In your paragraph, tell:

- some tree facts that you know.

- what you can do with a tree.

- if you like deciduous (trees that lose their leaves) or evergreen better. Give one or two reasons why.

- which tree you would visit and why if you could only visit either General Sherman or Methuselah (both very old trees).

General Sherman

giant sequoia

may be largest tree in the world

2,300–2,700 years old

about 275 feet tall

trunk almost 37 feet wide

California

Methuselah

bristlecone pine

may be oldest tree in the world

over 4,800 years old

about 55 feet tall

trunk about 4 ½ feet wide

California

_____

_____

_____

_____

_____

When Trees Were Young

DID YOU KNOW? How can you tell how old a tree is? You count its rings. A tree grows one ring for every year.

Activity: Imagine you lived 2,500 years ago when a tree called General Sherman was young. What would your day have been like? Write a paragraph about how you might spend your day. Tell what you might eat or wear. What might you do for fun? Remember, there is no electricity. There are no roads. The only people are hunter/gatherers.

_____

_____

_____

_____

_____

_____

_____

_____

_____

_____

_____

_____

_____

The Musician

Activity: Write a story in which you are a musician. You can play any type of instrument you want. Tell what instrument you play. Your instrument can be a real instrument or an imaginary one. Describe it. Tell what it sounds like. Explain how people or animals feel when they hear you play.

What you write cannot be wrong. It is your choice. So make your instrument real, funny, scary, or magical. It is all up to you!

Organization

The Fastest

Is it easier to figure out fastest to slowest in A or B?

A. The cheetah is fast. The lion is faster than the black mamba snake. The hyena is not slower than the zebra. Speeds go from 70 to 20 miles an hour (mph).

B. At 70 miles per hour (mph), the cheetah is the fastest land animal. The lion can run 50 mph. The hyena and the zebra can both run 40 mph. All these animals can outpace the black mamba snake that can only go 20 mph.

Activity: Write about animal speeds. You can go from slowest to fastest. You can go from fastest to slowest. Keep the order straight. This will help the reader understand. Make some of your sentences a bit different from the others. This will help make your reading interesting.

Animal	Speed (mph)
cheetah	70
pronghorn antelope	61
lion	50
quarter horse	47
elk	45
hyena	40
ostrich	40
zebra	40
black mamba snake	20

_____

_____

_____

_____

_____

The Race!

Activity: Imagine there is a race among a group of animals. You are the announcer. Write what you say during the race. When you write, think about what announcers say. Who will win? It is up to you! When you write, follow these steps:

First—introduce yourself.

Second—tell who is in the race.

Third—tell who is the crowd's favorite.

Fourth—start the race.

Fifth—describe some action that is going on—like who is passing, who is creeping up, and who is falling behind.

Sixth—tell the winner.

Animals in the Race	Speed (mph)
kangaroo	30
grizzly bear	30
white-tailed deer	30
elephant	25

_____

_____

_____

_____

_____

_____

_____

The Days of the Week

Sunday, Monday, Tuesday, Wednesday, Thursday, Friday, Saturday

Activity: You need to learn the days of the week. It is easier to learn them in order. Write a paragraph about the days of the week. When you write,

- first, tell what your paragraph is about.

- decide if Sunday or Monday is the first day of the week.

- write about each day, in order. Make your sentences a little different, so your writing is more interesting.

- start your sentences with or use words like **then comes, next, the first, the second, following, in between, after**, etc. These words help your writing flow smoothly.

Example: *After Tuesday comes Wednesday and Thursday. Wednesday and Thursday are the third and fourth days.*

_____

_____

_____

_____

_____

_____

_____

_____

_____

Potatoes All Week

Activity: Write a story about a child who plants potatoes. You pick the name of the child and the day. Then say what happens every day of the week in order.

Will the child water, hoe, pull up weeds, put on fertilizer, watch, or stop animals from eating the plants? You choose!

Make it so the potatoes are amazing. Everyone says they can't grow that fast, but they do! Have the child dig up the potatoes, make something out of them, and eat them. Will it be mashed potatoes, French fries, or potato salad? You choose!

All of this will happen in one week! That's what happens with amazing potatoes!

Story Start

THINK ABOUT IT!

What are some words or phrases that can be used to start a story?

What are some words or phrases that signal the end of a story?

Sometimes the writer starts the story with action to grab the reader's attention.

What sentence is most likely the beginning of a story?

a. A loud crash made Sammy leap out of bed.

b. Finally, after every spider was swept away, Sammy was able to crawl into bed.

Activity: Now it is your turn. Write about a time when you heard a crash or when you leapt out of bed. You can leap out of bed for many reasons. It might be because you heard a crash. It might be because of something you were going to do that day. It might be because it was your birthday. You choose!

_____

_____

_____

_____

_____

_____

_____

_____

_____

The Crow and the Water Pitcher

The lines below are the actions that take place in a story. They are in the wrong order. Number them so they are in the right order.

> __3__ Crow can't reach water in pitcher, even when puts head in.
>
> _____ Crow sees water pitcher.
>
> _____ At last Crow can drink because water level rises.
>
> __4__ Crow gets a stone and drops in.
>
> _____ Over and over Crow gets stones and drops in pitcher.
>
> _____ One day Crow is thirsty.

Actions in a story need to go in the proper order. This is so the story makes sense. There needs to be a clear beginning. There needs to be a clear ending.

Activity: Write up the tale of "The Crow and the Water Pitcher" in proper story order. Add details to and/or change words from the lines above. Use words that will make your sentences flow smoothly. Add details so that your story is more interesting.

_____

_____

_____

_____

_____

_____

_____

_____

Phone Manners

Organization

THINK ABOUT IT! When you call someone on the phone, what should you say? You should do three things. First, you should give a greeting. Second, you should say who you are. Third, you should ask to speak to someone. Don't forget to use the word "please!"

One of these greetings is perfect. Two have one thing wrong with them. Fix the ones that are wrong.

> **1.** Hello, this is Mindy. May I please speak to Mika?
>
> **2.** Yeah, this is Rick. May I please speak to Roxanne?
>
> **3.** Hi, this is Kendra. I want to speak to Kyle.

Activity: Now write down a phone conversation you might have with a friend. Make sure you start it off with the three things you should say when you call someone! Then invite the person to do something with you. Tell them **what**, **when**, and **where**. Tell them **why** they should come. Tell them **what** to bring. Make sure your conversation has a proper beginning and ending.

Format your conversation like this:

Name of person talking: what the person says

_____

_____

_____

_____

_____

_____

_____

_____

No Such Thing!

Activity: Think of a friend you like to call. Then write down an imaginary conversation with that friend. Start out by writing three things you should say when you call someone (give a greeting, say who you are, ask to speak to someone). Then tell your friend you have something. Give your friend hints. Have your friend guess what it is. Have your friend say things like, "There can't be any such thing!" Make the reader want to know what it is! Then finally tell your friend what it is.

What are you going to tell your friend you have? It is lighter than a feather, but it is harder to hold. It is your breath!

School Day

DID YOU KNOW?

School days are not the same all over the world. Some children go to a school, and some children learn at home. Some children wear uniforms and some children ride a bus. Some children bring their lunch and some children have art or music on special days.

Activity: Write about your school day. Before you write, plan ahead. Divide your day into three parts: **the beginning, the middle,** and **the end**. Write about each part in a separate paragraph. The first line in each paragraph should tell the reader what part of the day you will be talking about. You can talk about what you wear and how you get to school in the paragraph about the beginning part of your school day.

Remember—indent each paragraph!

_____

_____

_____

_____

_____

_____

_____

_____

_____

_____

_____

Dogs that Sniff

IMAGINE THAT!

Dogs can smell things that people can't. Some dogs are specially trained. Beagles are trained to work in airports. The beagles are trained to sniff out certain foods and plants, and even stowaway animals. The foods and plants may carry pests or diseases. Taking the foods and plants to a new place may help the pests or diseases spread. The stowaway animals may be stolen. So why are beagles used? Most people are not afraid of beagles. People think beagles are cute.

Activity: Imagine you are a beagle working in an airport. Describe what might happen during your day. What will you find? Are people surprised at what you do? Begin with the start of the day. End when the day is over. Use the word **I** since you are pretending to be the beagle.

_____

_____

_____

_____

_____

_____

_____

_____

_____

_____

Pet Problem

THINK ABOUT IT!

Many stories have problems. The problem may be that someone is lost or that someone needs to learn how to do something. The problem may be that people can't get along, that someone is told to do something he or she does not want to do, or that someone has been given something he or she does not want to have. At the end of the story, the problem is solved. People learn how to get along. The treasure is found. People find their way home or get what they want.

Activity: At times, there are problems with pets. Where do they belong? Think about what pets would be best in what places. Tell why and give examples. Before you write, plan ahead by jotting down the names of some kinds of pets under the headings:

apartment	house	farm

_____

_____

_____

_____

_____

_____

_____

_____

Zoo Escape!

Activity: Write a story in which there is a problem with an animal that has escaped from the zoo. Describe how you find the animal. Your story can be funny, scary, or serious. You choose!

Plan ahead by jotting down notes saying:

who is in the story

when the story takes place

where the story takes place

what the problem is

how the problem is solved

_____

_____

_____

_____

_____

_____

_____

_____

What Calf?

Activity: Some baby animals are called calves. A baby blue whale is a calf. Write a story about one of the calves below. Use some of the facts in your description.

Make sure your facts flow together by starting your sentences with words like:

> *One amazing fact is . . .*
>
> *It is hard to believe, but . . .*
>
> *Many people don't know, but . . .*
>
> *One interesting thing about this kind of calf is that . . .*

Blue whale calf	Elephant calf
• at birth, about 23 feet long • at birth, about 5,000 to 6,000 pounds • can drink 50 gallons of milk a day • gains 200 pounds a day its first year • weaned (stops drinking milk) at about six months • when weaned, about doubles in length! • one born at a time	• at birth, about 3 feet high • at birth, about 200–260 pounds • drinks about 3 gallons of milk a day • hairy with a long tail; short trunk • drinks mother's milk with mouth so doesn't need long trunk • weaned from 1 to 10 years • one born at a time

_____

_____

_____

_____

_____

_____

The Calf in the Barn

DID YOU KNOW? A baby moose is called a calf. A baby bison is a calf. So is a baby hippopotamus, camel, or giraffe. A baby cow is also called a calf.

Activity: Write a story that is set at a dairy farm. At a dairy farm, mother cows have baby calves all the time. Have someone come in and tell his or her parents that there is a new calf in the barn. Describe the calf. Have the parents think the child is joking. Then what do people find out? The calf is not the kind they thought it was!

What type of calf will it be? What does the calf do? What happens to the calf? It is up to you!

Crossing South Georgia Island

Activity: News reports tell who, what, where, when, why, and sometimes how. Use the facts to write a news report. Use words that make it exciting to read. When you write, tell how Shackleton solved a problem. Think of a good headline for your story, and make sure you include your byline. Think of a first sentence that draws your readers in.

Who: Shackleton, Worsley, and Crean

What: needed to stay awake or would freeze to death

Where: crossing snow-covered South Georgia Island to get help

When: May 1916, after being shipwrecked

Why: tired, hungry, thirsty, weak, no warm clothes or shelter

How: Shackleton forced himself to stay awake for five minutes. Then he woke others and said they had slept for half an hour!

Staying Awake

Activity: Imagine that you are going to the far north for the first time. You get there in the morning. Your mother says, "You can play until it gets dark." Your mother does not know that in the summer, the sun does not set. It is light 24 hours of the day! How long do you think you can play outside? What will you do to try and stay awake? How long do you think you can stay awake?

_____

_____

_____

_____

_____

_____

_____

_____

_____

_____

_____

Journey on Ice

DID YOU KNOW?

Shackleton left on December 5, 1914. It was **497** days before he and his men touched land again. Ten months after leaving, Shackleton's boat got caught in the ice. The ice crushed it, and it sank. The men lived on the ice pack. When they reached open water, they sailed in their tiny lifeboats. The men ate seals and penguins to survive.

Activity: We know a lot about Shackleton and his men because of the journals the men wrote. Fill in two of the journal entries for the men. When you write, think about what the men might have seen. Tell what they might have hoped for or how they might have felt.

December 25, 1914	December 25, 1915

Journey to Mars

IMAGINE THAT! Maybe one day you will be able to travel to Mars. Your rocket will go 25,000 miles an hour! That is fast, but it will still take seven to nine months. This is because Mars and Earth are not still. They are both moving.

Activity: Imagine you are on a spaceship to Mars. You will not touch land for months! When you land, you might shrink two inches! This is because in space there is little gravity. Your spine is like a spring, and nothing is pushing it down.

Write two journal entries. When you write, think about what you might see. Tell what you might hope for or how you might feel. Include at least one space fact in your entries.

Date _____

_____

_____

_____

_____

_____

_____

_____

_____

_____

_____

_____

Date _____

_____

_____

_____

_____

_____

_____

_____

_____

_____

_____

_____

Rhyming Poems

Some poems rhyme. The last words in each sentence or phrase have the same sound.

My Friend Jenny

Jenny has brown eyes,
I'm telling no lies.

She knows to say "please"
And not walk on her knees.

She brushes her hair
And always takes care.

When she sees a rat,
She sends her cat,

And that's that!

Shackleton the Explorer

Shackleton went to the ice,
Where he found it wasn't always so nice.

His boat, it did sink,
That would make most people think
That the end was near.

Shackleton just said, "Never fear.
We're out of here!"

Activity: Write a rhyming poem about a real person, place, or thing. Your poem can be silly or serious. Write at least six lines, or three rhyming pairs.

_____

_____

_____

_____

_____

_____

_____

_____

The Cheebra

Writing can be very creative and fun, especially when you make things up. There is no such thing as a cheebra. Still, you can write a rhyming poem about it that is fun to say. You can also write rhyming poems about other made-up animals, places, or things.

The Cheebra

The cheebra
Is quite different from a zebra.

It has no stripes, just spots
Of pink and purple dots.

When it eats a berry,
It becomes quite merry.

It would be quite fun
To own one!

The Planet Tooper

There is a planet named Tooper,
It really is quite super.

When children go to school,
They jump into a pool.

When they learn about other lands,
They walk on their hands.

The teacher is a polar bear,
And no one can be wrong there.

Activity: Make up your own rhyming poem. Your poem can be silly or serious. Write at least six lines, or three rhyming pairs.

_____

_____

_____

_____

_____

_____

_____

Captain Cook

Activity: Captain Cook was a British explorer. He created many maps and was the first European to sail to lots of places. Look at the list of places Cook explored on his first trip. Weave them into a paragraph. Use the following sentences:

First sentence: tell what the paragraph is about.

Middle sentences: tell in order where he went. Make some sentences long and others short. Tie the sentences together with joining words such as: **next, after, this stop was followed by, continuing on his journey, before heading home.**

Last sentence: say something about Cook being a great explorer, still famous today, or also known for two other daring trips

Cook's Trip

1. left England August, 1768 on ship *Endeavor*
2. Rio de Janeiro, Brazil, South America
3. Tahiti
4. New Zealand
5. east coast of Australia
6. Indonesia
7. Cape of Good Hope at southern tip of Africa
8. back to England July, 1771

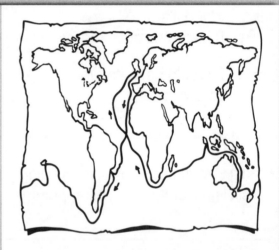

Can you trace Cook's route on a map?

_____

_____

_____

_____

_____

Treasure Hunt

Activity: Imagine that you are setting up a treasure hunt. Your hunt should be in your school or in your house and yard. It should have at least five stops.

> **First** sentence: tell what the paragraph is about.
>
> **Middle** sentences: give the clues. Use words like **next, then,** and **after** to make your writing flow smoothly.
>
> **Last** sentence: tell how one should feel or describe the treasure.

You can have fun with your clues! For example, instead of a swing, you can say, "Your second clue is under the thing where you pump your legs to go up and down!"

_____

_____

_____

_____

_____

_____

_____

_____

_____

_____

_____

_____

Raining Frogs

Activity: Can it rain frogs? Yes, it can! Weave the following information into a paragraph. Try to make your first sentence exciting. Use an example. Where should your example go? You choose! It can go near the start, middle, or end of your paragraph. How will you conclude your story? You might write about what you hope to see one day.

> **What**: frogs raining from sky
>
> **How**: picked up in waterspouts or strong winds that resemble a tornado and carried far away
>
> **Why**: frogs are very light
>
> **When**: throughout history
>
> **Where**: reports from around the world

Example: Odzacai, Serbia, 2005. Frogs not from the area rained down. Then they hopped all over town looking for water.

_____

_____

_____

_____

_____

_____

_____

_____

_____

Raining Fish

IMAGINE THAT!

Believe it or not, it is not just frogs that can fall from the sky. Sometimes fish do, too!

Activity: Imagine you get rained on by fish. Write a paragraph about it. Tell where you are, whom you are with, what you are doing, and when it happens. Tell what you see, feel, and do. Do people believe you? What do you do with the fish?

One day I _____

_____

_____

_____

_____

_____

_____

_____

_____

_____

_____

_____

_____

Blast Off!

Ten . . nine . . eight . . seven . . . six . . five . . four . . three . . . two . . . one . . blast off!

Activity: Blast off to what? You decide! Count down from ten. Write what you should do or check as you count down—one thing for each number. You can do this for something real. (For example: getting ready for school, making breakfast, or painting a picture) You can do this for something imaginary. (For example: feeding your pet dinosaur, jumping to the top of a tree, or acting in a movie)

Think about the order. It would not make sense to put your socks on before your shoes!

Ten_____

_____

Nine_____

_____

Eight_____

_____

Seven_____

_____

Six_____

_____

Five_____

_____

Four_____

_____

Three_____

_____

Two_____

_____

One_____

_____

Blast off!

Conventions

A Capital Idea

What is wrong with these sentences?

el capitan is a huge rock. It is in yosemite valley, california. mike corbett carried mark wellman from his wheelchair to the rock base on wednesday, july 19. The two men were going to climb el capitan! It took them over a week. At night they dangled in sleeping bags thousands of feet above the yosemite valley floor. mike climbed first and set up ropes. Then mark pulled himself up the ropes.

Circle what is missing: periods or capital letters.

Go back and fix the paragraph. Use the numbers to help you find all the mistakes.

> What should have capital letters? (17 total)
>
> Days and months 2   Names of people 6
>
> Names of places or mountains 9

Activity: Now show what you know! Write a short paragraph with at least four sentences about something you or someone else did. Have missing capitals for at least one person, day, month, and place. Then write the paragraph correctly on the back of this page.

Show your test paragraph to your classmates. Could they spot the words that needed capital letters?

_____

_____

_____

_____

_____

_____

_____

Song and Movie Names

THINK ABOUT IT! Song and movie names all start with capital letters. The little words like *a, in, on, and,* or *the* do not—unless they are the first or last word!

Put song titles in quotes (" ").

Underline handwritten movie titles. (Typewritten ones can be in italics.)

Example: In the movie <u>Up in a Balloon</u>, Joey sings the song "Happy Birthday."

Correct the sentences below. Put in capital letters (12), underline movie titles (1), and put song titles in quotes (2).

> On tuesday, I sang the star spangled banner to mr. big's class.
>
> No one sings old macDonald had a farm in the movie toy story.

Activity: Now, imagine that one day you will write, direct, or star in a movie. Write a few sentences in which you tell:

- what the name of the movie will be.
- the name of a character in the movie.
- a place where the story might take place.
- what day or month something might happen.
- the name of a song (made up or real) that is sung in the movie.

Remember—underline your movie title! Put your song title in quotes. Use capital letters for names, places, and days of the week and month.

_____

_____

_____

_____

_____

_____

Facts About Butterflies

Read the three sentences. Then put a period (.), question mark (?), or exclamation point (!) at the end.

1. How does a butterfly taste things

2. A butterfly does not taste things the same way you do

3. As incredible as it sounds, a butterfly tastes with its feet

Correct the following sentences by putting in 5 periods (.), 1 question mark (?), and 1 exclamation point (!).

What does a butterfly have that it can coil up like a rope___ It has a proboscis__ The proboscis is a long hollow tube___ When a butterfly wants to eat, it uncoils its proboscis___ It sticks it deep into a flower__ Then it sucks up nectar___ You could say the proboscis is like a long, rolled-up straw___

Activity: Now write at least three sentences about butterflies. Use facts from the box. Use at least one period, one question mark, and one exclamation point.

Butterflies

- biggest has a wingspan of 11 inches
- smallest could fit on the top of your nose
- females duller (this helps them blend in and be safe from predators when laying eggs)
- smell with antennae

_____

_____

_____

_____

_____

A Big Surprise

IMAGINE THAT!

There is an egg. What hatches out? A caterpillar does! The caterpillar's outer skin hardens. It turns into a chrysalis. What comes out? A butterfly comes out!

Activity: Imagine that someone does not know this. Write a story about this person. Is the person upset in your story? Is the person surprised? What does the person think has happened to the caterpillar? Is it lost? Has it been stolen?

Use at least one period, question mark, and one exclamation point in your story.

When you are done, check your story. Did you remember to use periods, question marks, and exclamation points?

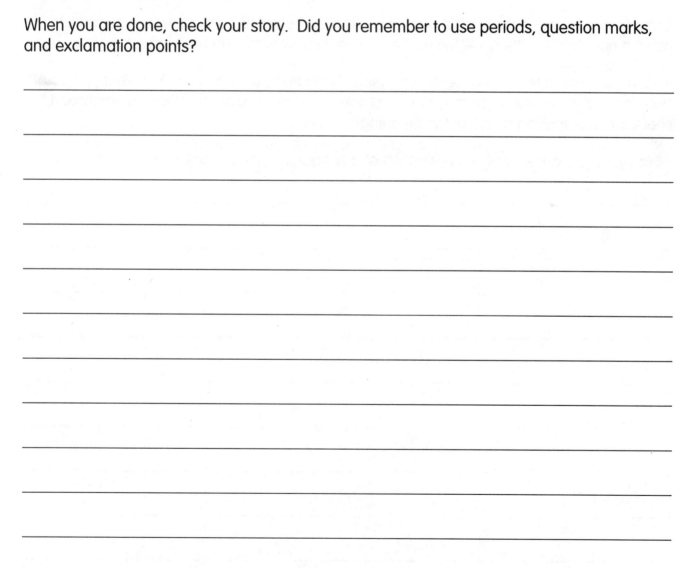

What Hour Is Our Train?

> What train is coming? Is it our train? Oh, yes, it is our train. We had better get on quickly because our train leaves when the clock strikes the hour. We will be on our train for an hour or more.

Go back to the sentences above. Circle these words: our (4) and hour (2).

Do the words **our** and **hour** sound the same?

a. no   **b.** yes

Are the words **our** and **hour** spelled the same?

a. no   **b.** yes

Some words sound the same but are not spelled the same. When you write, you have to use the right word. Otherwise the reader may not know what you really mean.

Activity: Write at least three sentences using the words *our* and *hour*. Tell what you do or don't do in our classroom, school, house, or table and at what hour. When you are done, check that the spelling matches the meaning!

Example: We do not walk on our hands at any hour in our classroom.

_____

_____

_____

_____

_____

_____

_____

_____

Glass Panes

> The window has a colored pane of glass.
>
> Sally felt a stab of pain when she stepped on the stick.

Write down one word from each sentence above. The words are not spelled the same, but they sound the same. They start with "p."

1. _____   **2.** _____

Do the sentences below make sense?

> The window has a colored pain of glass.
>
> Sally felt a stab of pane when she stepped on the stick.

1. no   **2.** yes

Find and correct the 4 misspelled words below.

The first windows had no glass pains. They were covered with animal hide, cloth, or wood. Some pains were made of flattened animal horns. What a pane it must have been not to have glass pains. It would have been hard to see because little light could enter.

Activity: Now think about the words **know** and **no**. What if you had a friend who could not speak English? How could you **know** if the person was saying yes or **no**? How could you **know** you had understood correctly? Write down how you **know**. Make sure you use the words **know** and **no**. When you are done, check that the spelling matches the meaning.

_____

_____

_____

_____

_____

_____

The Tallest Mountain

DID YOU KNOW? When you write, you need to check your spelling. If you spell words correctly, the reader will know what you mean. There is a list of 100 words. The list has words that are hard to spell. The words on the list are spelled wrong all the time. What words are on the list? One word is *believe*.

Correct the spelling in the following sentences: (5 words)

> Some beleive that Mt. Everest is the tallest mountain. Others do not beleive this. They beleive that Mt. Mauna Kea is the tallest. How high is Mt. Everest? It is 29,035 feet above sea level. How high is Mt. Mauna Kea? It is only 13,796 feet above sea level. Yet some beleive it is taller. Why? Mt. Mauna Kea starts lower. It starts at the bottom of the seafloor. From bottom to top, it is over 32,800 feet! What do you beleive? It is up to you.

Activity: Write down what mountain you believe is the tallest in the world. Tell why. Use the word **believe** at least one time.

Think: Some people believe the *tallest* and the *highest* are not the same thing.

_____

_____

_____

_____

_____

_____

_____

_____

_____

_____

Under the Bed

Activity: Make up a story in which someone talks about what is under his or her bed. Describe it in detail. It can be something like a lion or a made-up creature. Have other people say over and over that they do not believe it. Then, at the end of the story, have the thing under the bed come out!

Remember to use the word **believe**!

When you are done, read over what you wrote. Check your spelling. Check your capital letters. Check the ends of your sentences.

_____

_____

_____

_____

_____

_____

_____

_____

_____

_____

_____

It's or Its

DID YOU KNOW? The words *it's* and *its* are on a list. What is the list? The list is of words people often misspell. *It's* and *its* do not mean the same thing. You want people to know what you mean, so you want to use the right word.

It's means "it is" or "it has."

It's late so I will go to bed.

Its is the possessive form of "it." If you possess something, it belongs to you. It is yours

I like its tail.

The rule: if you can say "it is" or "it has," use it's.

Correct the spelling in the following sentences.

Its time to blow out the candles. (Can you say "it is"?)

It's house is the blue one. (Can you say "it is"?)

Activity: Name four animals. Then say something about what each animal has. Use the words **it's** and **its** at least one time for each animal.

Example: It's a tiger. Its stripes are even on its skin!

1. _____

_____

2. _____

_____

3. _____

_____

4. _____

_____

Go back and check your spelling. Can you use "it is" or "it has"? If so, it should be spelled *it's.*

The Note

THINK ABOUT IT!

Crow got a note. The note said, "Son, its time to send me more money."

Crow took the note to Detective Dog. Crow said, "This note did not come from my mother."

Detective Dog said, "How do you know? I don't know how you can tell."

Activity: Tell why Crow knew the note did not come from his mother.

Hint: Crow's mother was an English teacher. What word would she never misspell?

Then have Crow teach Detective Dog how to check if it should be **it's** or **its**.

Big, Bigger, Biggest

THINK ABOUT IT!

The Indian Ocean is big. The Atlantic Ocean is bigger. The Pacific Ocean is the biggest.

The Indian Ocean is deep. The Atlantic Ocean is deeper. The Pacific Ocean is the deepest.

Using words like *big, bigger,* and *biggest* helps the reader form a picture in his or her head. It helps the reader compare things.

Activity: Write four sets of comparisons about

1. kinds of food: good, better, best

2. sticky things: sticky, stickier, stickiest

3. different states: far, farther, farthest

4. jokes: fun, funnier, funniest

_____

_____

_____

_____

_____

_____

_____

_____

_____

_____

The Tallest Tale

Activity: A tall tale is not true. It is made up. Write a dialogue. In your dialogue, have a boy and a girl tell tall tales. The tales should be about what they saw on the street. No matter what one person says, the other person saw something that was bigger, smaller, prettier, or scarier. Use your imagination when it comes to what they talk about.

> I saw a dog as <u>big</u> as a bus.
>
> Is that all? I saw the biggest dog. It was bigger than a plane!

_____

_____

_____

_____

_____

_____

_____

_____

_____

_____

_____

How do we know what someone is saying in stories? We put their words in quotation marks
(" "). We add commas (,) to separate their words from the rest of the sentence.

Look at the example. Circle the commas and quotation marks.

> *Calvin Coolidge was president. He didn't talk much. One time, a lady said, "I made
> a bet that I can get you to say at least than three words."*

Did the comma go before or after the quotation marks?

Did the period go before or after the quotation marks?

Now, fix the following sentence. Put in these marks: **? , " . "**

> *What did Calvin say He said You lose*

Activity: Now it is your turn to write! Write a paragraph.

First lines: Say who Coolidge was and what he said. Use this quote: "I have never been
hurt by what I have not said."

Middle: Tell what you think Coolidge meant.

End: Use an example from your own life when being quiet was a good thing, or a time
when you would have been better off keeping quiet.

_____

_____

_____

_____

_____

_____

_____

Talking About . . .

Activity: Write a conversation between two people. The conversation can be about riddles, pets, or the weather. It can be about what they will see, do, or wear. It is up to you.

When you write, change the start of your sentences by using words like *said, yelled, cried, screamed, whispered,* or *answered* before your quotes.

Example: Kellie yelled, "I can't believe you just said that!"

Now go back and read what you wrote. Check your commas and quotation marks!

_____

_____

_____

_____

_____

_____

_____

_____

_____

_____

_____

_____

What the Rhino Knows

I'm not seen. I'm close, but I am not seen. He's not seen. He's close, but he is not seen. She's not seen. She's close, but she is not seen. They're not seen. They're close, but they are not seen. We're not seen. We're close, but we are not seen. That's because rhinos have bad eyesight. That is because rhinos have bad eyesight. What do they have to make up for the bad eyesight? They have a very good sense of smell.

Write down the words that are different in the sentences:

1. I'm not seen. I am not seen. ___I'm, I am___

2. He's not seen. He is not seen._____

3. She's not seen. She is not seen._____

4. They're not seen. They are not seen._____

5. We're not seen. We are not seen._____

6. That's because rhinos . . . That is because rhinos . . . _____

Make the punctuation mark you use for the missing letters: _____

Activity: Write sentences in which you tell how you are close to a rhino. Tell how another person is hundreds of feet away. Tell why the rhino knows the faraway person is there but doesn't know you are there.

Hint: The faraway person is upwind. You are downwind.

Use at least two of these words in your sentences:

I'm, he's, she's, they're, we're, that's

Go back and read what you wrote. Did you put in an apostrophe (') for the missing letters?

_____

_____

_____

_____

It's Gone!

Activity: Write a short story about a rhino that gets its horn knocked off. Have the rhino cry, "It's gone!" and "It is gone!"

Weave these rhino horn facts into your story:

A rhino's horn:

- is thickly matted hair.
- is made of keratin (the same thing your hair and fingernails are made of).
- never stops growing.
- can grow one to three inches a year.

When you are done, go back and read what you wrote. Did you remember all of your punctuation marks?

_____

_____

_____

_____

_____

_____

_____

What Island?

THINK ABOUT IT!

Does spelling matter? Does writing clearly matter? Oh, yes, they do! Write down the letters that make up these two countries in the spaces below.

Ireland   Iceland

__ __ __ __ __ __ __   __ __ __ __ __ __ __

What is the only difference? _____

Activity: Write two short paragraphs. Write about Ireland in one paragraph and Iceland in the other. Use what you know and facts from the fact box. Tell what place you would rather go to and why.

Ireland	Iceland
island	island
mild climate	glaciers
often rains	active volcanoes
no snakes	geysers
close to Great Britain	dark and freezing cold in winter
lots of castles	no snakes

Read over what you wrote. Did you remember to indent the start of each paragraph?

_____

_____

_____

_____

_____

Travel Shock

Activity: Write a story with at least two paragraphs. The first paragraph should be about a person who wants to go to Iceland or Ireland. You choose which place. Tell why the person wants to go there. The person buys a ticket. The problem is messy handwriting or sloppy typing. The wrong ticket gets bought!

The second paragraph is about when the person finds out. You decide when and how the person finds out. Is the person angry or surprised? Does it take a while before the person finds out he or she is on the wrong island? What does the person do?

When you are done, go back and read your writing. Check for neatness and spelling. Make sure you indented each paragraph. Add a title.

The Longest Hiccups

You can make two short sentences into one long one by doing three things.

1. Put a comma (,) after the first sentence.
2. add the words **and**, **or**, or **but**.
3. change the first letter of the second sentence into a lowercase letter, unless it is a proper noun.

> *Example:*
>
> Charles Osborne began to hiccup in 1922.
>
> He hiccupped until 1990.
>
> Charles Osborn began to hiccup in 1922, and he hiccupped until 1990!

Where is the comma? _____

Which words connect the two sentences? _____

Turn these two sentences into one with the word **but**:

    He hiccupped up to 40 times a minute the first decade.

    He slowed down to 20 times a minute in later years.

_____

> **Activity:** Write two short sentences about two countries you would like to go visit. Then combine them into one sentence using the word **or**.

short: _____

short: _____

long: _____

_____

> Now write two short sentences of your own. Then make them into one long one using **and**, **or**, or **but**.

short: _____

short: _____

long: _____

_____

When you are done, go back and read your long sentence. Did you remember the comma?

Stop the Hiccups!

Activity: Write a story about a boy or girl. The boy or girl cannot stop hiccupping. Tell what happens to him or her. When did the hiccups start? Do the hiccups ever stop? What stops them?

When you write, make at least two long sentences by putting two short sentences together with **and, or,** or **but**.

When you are done, go back and read what you wrote. Check your spelling. Check your punctuation. Did you remember to put the comma before **and, or,** or **but** when you joined two complete sentences?

Goose, Gooses, or Geese

When you write, you put a comma after **someone's name** or words like **sir**, **madam**, **yes**, **no**, **hi**, or **hello** when they start a sentence.

Example:

Pat, if there is more than one goose, you do not say "gooses." You say "geese."

No, you do not say "mouses." You say "mice" if there is more than one mouse.

Activity: Write some sentences in which you tell people the word to use for more than one child, man, woman, foot, and tooth.

Start each sentence with a word that needs a comma after it. The word can be a **name** or **sir**, **madam**, **yes**, **no**, **hi**, or **hello**.

_____

_____

_____

_____

_____

_____

_____

_____

_____

_____

_____

Buy It!

Activity: Imagine you are a salesperson. Choose what you are selling. Practice your selling by making up lines between you and customers.

Sir, I have just the thing you need!

When you write:

- start each line with a short word that needs a comma after it.

- make your product sound the best.

- make it sound as if your product is a must-have!

When you are done, go back and read what you wrote. Did you remember all your commas?

_____

_____

_____

_____

_____

_____

_____

_____

_____

_____

Proofreading Marks

DID YOU KNOW?

Proofreading is when you read over what you wrote. You check for mistakes. How do proofreaders say what is wrong? They use certain marks. These are some of the marks:

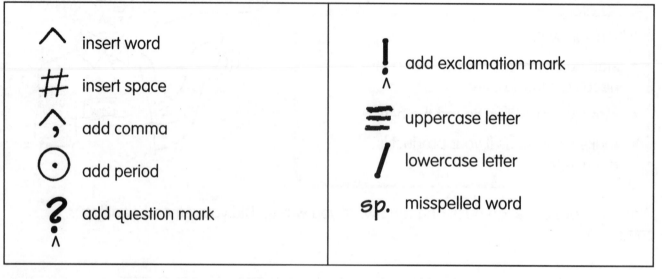

Add the proofreading marks needed below.

1 question mark, 2 misspelled words, 2 uppercase letters, 3 lowercase letters, 1 period, 1 insert space

> what do sea otters have They have Thick hair. They can have a million hairs in one square Inch! All this Hair helps keep a sea otttter warm. A seaotter fluffs up its hair. air gets trapped under the hair. The air helps the sea otter float. It helps the seea otter stay warm, too

Activity: Now show what you know! Write some sentences about your hair. Tell what it looks like. Tell how you like to wear it. Make some mistakes in your sentences. Mark the mistakes with the correct proofreading marks.

_____

_____

_____

_____

Tied up in Kelp!

Add 4 proofreading marks where needed:

did you no that baby otters are called pups
Kelp is a kind of seaweed

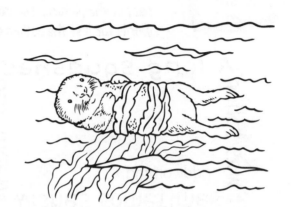

Activity: Now write a story about a person who sees an otter tied up in kelp. The person thinks the otter needs help. The otter does not need help! Mother otters use kelp as a babysitter! They wrap their pups in it so they won't float away.

When you are done with your story, go back and make five mistakes. Then put proofing marks by the mistakes.

_____

_____

_____

_____

_____

_____

_____

_____

_____

_____

Picture Poetry

DID YOU KNOW?

A picture poem is a kind of poem. A picture poem is a poem that is written in the shape of a picture. Your poem can be the outline of what you are writing about. It can be part of the picture. For example, if you did a picture poem of a rectangle, you could have words for just the outline or words that fill the entire rectangle.

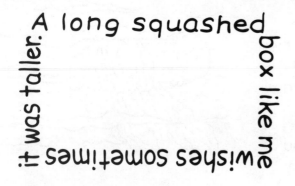

Activity: Write your own picture poem. Have fun with words, and have fun with shapes!

Writing Prompts

Prompt 1

You get to go back in time and meet someone. Who would you go meet? What would you ask? What would you do? Why did you want to see this person?

Prompt 2

I looked at the box on the table. It was addressed to me, but who could have sent it? I went to open it, but then suddenly . . .

Prompt 3

More vanilla ice cream is sold than any other flavor. Second is chocolate. Why do you think this is so? What is your favorite flavor? What is your least favorite flavor? If you could make a new ice-cream flavor, what would it be? What could you say that would make people want to buy it?

Prompt 4

For three hours you can either fly like a bird or swim like a fish. Which would you pick and why?

Prompt 5

Everyone stayed away from the house at the end of the street. Why?

Prompt 6

Your choice—you get to take a trip down the Amazon or the Nile River. Which one and why? What do you think you might see?

Prompt 7

I didn't think there was anything strange about the girl who sat down next to me on the bus until . . .

Prompt 8

You are talking to someone who has never seen a table before. Describe a table for the person. Tell what it looks like and what it is for.

Prompt 9

Think of all the stories you have read. You get to go into one! What story will you go into? Tell about an adventure you might have there.

Prompt 10

New words are being added to the English language every year. For example, the word "ringtone" was added to the dictionary in 2006. Make up a new word. Tell what it means. Then use it in a sentence. Your word can be silly, strange, or practical.

Prompt 11

My skin crawled and my hair stood on end when . . .

Prompt 12

You get to go back to a place that you really liked. Where will you go? Why do you want to go back? What will you do there?

Prompt 13

Suddenly, without warning, the lights went out.

Prompt 14

There are lots of holidays. Which one is your favorite? Why? Is there something special you do on that day?

Prompt 15

I was climbing a tree when all of sudden I heard a tiny voice say, "Watch out!" It was a talking _____.

Prompt 16

One day you will be in the Olympic Games. In which sport would you like to compete? Tell why. How would you get ready?

Prompt 17

You are given one thousand dollars to give away. To whom would you give the money and why?

Prompt 18

Could the treasure map be real?

Prompt 19

You are in charge of building a playground. What would you put in it? Where would the play equipment, courts, or pools go? What would be next to, behind, or close to each other?

Prompt 20

Your friend or someone else you know is feeling sad. How could you cheer them up?

Prompt 21

"That's the key," my friend whispered. "That's the one everyone is looking for. Now, do we dare _____ ?"

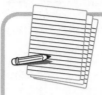

Prompt 22

You get to take a trip to see a bear. Would you rather see a polar bear in the Arctic or a spectacled bear in South America? Tell why.

Prompt 23

There are two new baby hippos, one new panda bear, and three baby giraffes. You get to name them! You want names that people will like but will also fit the animals. What will you name the hippos, panda bear, and giraffes? Why do you think they are good names?

Prompt 24

Linda had never been more tired in her life, but she knew she could not stop.

Prompt 25

Sometimes tickets have different prices. Children and seniors pay less. Is this fair? Why do you agree or disagree? Where is it okay or not okay to have different prices?

Prompt 26

You are teaching someone manners. Give one or two examples each of the times when one should say, "please," "thank you," and "excuse me."

Prompt 27

"Thump!" Max was so startled by the loud sound that he almost forgot to breathe.

Prompt 28

You can travel across the ocean on a submarine, plane, ship, or raft. Which one would you choose and why? Why might someone choose something different than you did?

Prompt 29

Finally, the day had arrived! Sandy was going to . . .

Prompt 30

Your school is being repainted. You get to pick the paint colors for the cafeteria, library, halls, kindergarten, and your classroom. What colors will you pick? Why?

Prompt 31

You're a star! What type of star would you like to be and why? You could be an actor, a singer, or a sports player. Tell some of the good and bad things that might come from being a star.

Prompt 32

One morning you see an odd-looking cookie on the table. You take a bite out of it, and all of a sudden you begin to tingle. Then, much to your surprise, you . . .

Prompt 33

One evening you realize that you can see in the dark as well as when it is light. Would you tell people? What things could you do? What jobs would you be good at?

Prompt 34

How are you different from an elephant?

Prompt 35

Once upon a time, there was a cheetah who wanted stripes instead of spots.

Prompt 36

You are going to be stranded on an island for one year. What four things will you take with you and why?

176